THE **NiA** GUIDE FOR BLACK WOMEN
Achieving Career Success
On Your Terms

Enjoy Success on Your Terms!

Cheryl Mayberry McKissack

THE NiA GUIDE FOR BLACK WOMEN

Achieving Career Success On Your Terms

EDITED BY SHERYL HUGGINS
AND
CHERYL MAYBERRY McKISSACK

AGATE

Chicago

Printed in Canada.

Library of Congress Cataloging-in-Publication Data

The Nia guide for black women : achieving career success on your terms / edited by Sheryl Huggins & Cheryl Mayberry McKissack.
p. cm.
ISBN 1-932841-01-6 (pbk.)
1. African American women in the professions. 2. Career development. 3. Vocational guidance for women. 4. Vocational guidance for minorities. I. Huggins, Sheryl. II. McKissack, Cheryl Mayberry.

HD6054.2.U6N53 2004
650.1'082--dc22
      2004017185

10 9 8 7 6 5 4 3 2 1

Agate books are available in bulk at discount prices.
For more information, go to agatepublishing.com.

Learn more about all of the Nia Guides for Black Women
at www.niaonline.com.

From Cheryl: I must thank my husband Eric McKissack for his unconditional love and support, my Nia "family" who inspire me every day, and my mom, Thelma Mayberry Arnold, who taught me the real meaning of "purpose."

From Sheryl: My journey to this place has been wondrous, full of unexpected and rewarding turns. Many thanks to my mother, Angela Huggins, for pointing me in the right direction and shining a light to guide me; to my sister, Gail Huggins Porter, for providing loving "roadside assistance" when I needed it; and to my late father, David Huggins, for teaching me how to get here on my own terms.

Contents

INTRODUCTION & ACKNOWLEDGEMENTS

If you've cracked open this book, then chances are you're not entirely satisfied with where you are in your career.

You could be an ambitious intern with her sights set on the corner office. Maybe, after years of unsatisfying work, you've decided to finally go after your dream career, but you're not sure how to hit the ground running. Or perhaps you're determined that this is the year that you won't get passed over for that deserved promotion. To that, we'd like to remind you of the old saying: be careful what you wish for . . .

Take Teresa Kay-Aba Kennedy. As an undergraduate at Wellesley College she was named one of *Glamour* magazine's "Top 10 College Women in America." She went on to earn an MBA at Harvard University, and by the tender age of twenty-seven she was vice president of business development and operations at MTV Networks Interactive in New York City.

It looked like she had it all. Or, in retrospect as she might tell you, it all had her.

"My family literally could find me at the office at 1:30 in the morning on a Saturday," she confides. "I was constantly running, running, running. I was on the road all the time doing deals, basically. It turns out that my body couldn't keep up with me." One day at a business conference she began to have stomach pains. The pains eventually led to a ten-day hospital stay, during which she nearly died from a stress-induced ulcerated digestive system. "Even then I was shooting off orders [to colleagues] from the hospital," she quips.

But it wasn't until a few years later that Kennedy decided enough was enough. She left her lucrative, decade-long media career to become a yoga teacher, entrepreneur, and wellness activist. Though most people thought she had lost her mind, she says she had in fact found herself.

Now, at thirty-five, she is president of Power Living Enterprises, Inc., a multimedia lifestyle company offering inspirational content, lifestyle coaching and training services, motivational products from affirmation cards to CDs, and networking events. She recently shared her story with participants of the 2004 Nia Enterprises Leadership Summit in New York, during a session entitled "Enjoy the Climb."

Now she is enjoying her career on her own terms. We, the editors of NiaOnline (www.niaonline.com), created this book, *The Nia Guide for Black Women: Achieving Career Success on Your Terms*, so that you can too. Whether you want to leave behind the corporate grind, remake it in your own image, or simply move forward with your identity and sanity intact, this guide is for you.

Since October 2000, NiaOnline's comprehensive coverage of issues concerning black women and their families has included expert career development and life coaching advice, plus profiles of successful corporate queens, sister CEOs, civic soldiers, and ordinary women who dared to follow their dreams. All of it has been focused on helping black women not only to achieve success, but to enjoy it; not only to gain power, but to "bring purpose to power" (the theme of our annual Leadership Summit Series).

The concept of purpose is very dear to us at NiaOnline—in fact, it is the source of our name (*nia* means "purpose" in Swahili). If you're looking for a truly satisfying career—one on your own terms—then purpose must be the organizing principle, the one that shapes those terms. It's the common thread binding all of the topics covered in this book.

Focusing on your purpose is never a luxury, though at times it may seem like one—especially if you're "the only one" in your office. Then, your only focus may be to get ahead with your sanity intact. Exactly forty years after Title VII of the Civil Rights Act of 1964 prohibited employment discrimination based on race, color, religion, sex, or national origin, black women still have only a toehold on the ladder of success.

How This Guide Works

Do you have what it takes to achieve career success on your own terms?

The Nia Guide for Black Women is meant to help as many black women as possible increase their awareness of their professional possibilities and help them break any glass ceilings they encounter. In the following chapters, we here at Nia Enterprises hope you will find the resources and information you need not only to succeed in your career, but also to become a leader.

According to a 2002 U.S. Department of Labor, Bureau of Labor Statistics, Current Population Survey, more than a quarter of the 8 million black women employed in the U.S. now hold executive, managerial, administrative, or professional positions. However, only 106 out of nearly 14,000 Fortune 500 corporate officers were black women in 2002, according to a Catalyst Inc. survey. The glass ceiling that white women (14 percent of Fortune 500 corporate officers) encounter in their climb to the top is far less opaque than for us, and before cracking our skulls, the climb can be a very lonely one.

Part 1 of this guide, "Sole Sister: Keeping Your Pride and Sanity," addresses how to cope with being a minority in the workplace, how to thrive without losing your cultural identity, and how to shatter that glass ceiling.

Of course, a key part of career success is understanding the game, and knowing how to play it effectively. In Part 2, "A Sister's Map to the Corporate Minefield," we cover how to face discrimination, avoid traps that can sabotage your career, make the system work for you, and get paid what you're really worth. Given the fact that black women earn 86 percent of what white women earn, and a mere 68 percent of what white men earn ("Highlights of Women's Earnings in 2002," U.S. Department of Labor's Bureau of Labor Statistics), and black women managers make a paltry 58 cents for every dollar white male managers make (Catalyst Inc.) chances are you'll benefit from that last piece of advice.

Of course, part of making people value you is knowing how to develop and sell yourself, which is covered in Part 3, "Tips for Taking It to the Next Level."

Finally, no one becomes a success completely on her own. One of the top women in the ethnic haircare industry, Candace S. Matthews (president of the SoftSheen-Carson division of L'Oréal), counseled participants in the 2004 Nia Enterprises Leadership Summit in Chicago that leaders are created by a combination of performance (10 percent), image (60 percent) and exposure (30 percent). The need for exposure was not lost on minority women corporate managers who were surveyed by Catalyst in 1999. Nearly half of them cited the lack of an influential mentor or sponsor as an impediment to their success. This mirrors a NiaOnline poll in which 59 percent of respondents indicated they have never had a mentor (though interestingly, 64 percent of those responding to a later poll said they have at some point mentored someone else). In Part 4, "Create Your Own Old Girl's Network," we advocate a do-it-yourself approach to building your professional network, with advice on the art of effective networking, finding a mentor, and bringing purpose to your personal power by becoming one.

The Nia Story

The Nia Guide for Black Women is the culmination of a journey begun four years ago by Cheryl Mayberry McKissack, the founder, president, and CEO of Nia Enterprises LLC. A technology executive who herself felt the need to regain control of her career path on her own terms, McKissack saw the need for an agent to connect black women to 1) each other, 2) empowering advice, and 3) the companies that market to black families. It couldn't have launched at a less auspicious time—October 2000, the middle of the dot-com bust—but our sense of purpose and our dynamic membership of black women have carried us through to the present day.

During the past four years we've reached aspiring black women with advice for improving their lives at work and at home, through our website, NiaOnline, and events like the Leadership Summit Series. Through our ongoing research into the views and preferences of black women and their families, we've also gained expertise on your unique concerns. We're excited to address those concerns for a larger group of black women through this book, and others to follow.

Instrumental in the launch of Nia Enterprises and NiaOnline were our former COO, Bonita Coleman Stewart; our founding editor-in-chief, Stephanie Stokes Oliver; and our current chief technology officer, Darcy Prather. A year after the launch, Sheryl Huggins took over as executive editor, later gaining the titles of editor-in-chief and director of information services. Stephanie, and later Sheryl, supervised the editorial staff and group of writers without whom this book would not be possible. You are reading the product of their countless hours of research, writing, and lost sleep.

The editors, writers, and speakers who contributed to material from which this book is adapted include Teresa Ridley, Carolyn M. Brown, Harriette Cole, Hilary Beard, Patricia Winans of Magna Securities, Daphne Jones of Johnson & Johnson, Jennifer Lewis-Hall of The Journey Productions, and Teresa Kay-Aba Kennedy of Power Living Enterprises.

Also supporting this effort are Nia Enterprises' vice president of sales and marketing, Heather Davis; commu-

nications manager, Jessica Willis; and office manager/
assistant to the CEO, Yvette Shelby.

Acknowledgements and Thanks

Our many thanks to this guide's publisher, Doug Seibold,
president of Agate Publishing in Chicago. He saw the
potential in it almost before we did, and never flagged in
his enthusiasm or dedication to it. We'd also like to recognize the book's editor, Patrick Lohier, for whipping all of
the information we threw at him into excellent shape.

We would also like to thank the entire NiaOnline family of
editors, writers, and support personnel (for the sake of space
we have decided not to name those who did not contribute
directly to this book, but their dedication to the Nia ideal has
nonetheless made this book possible); our families; our
friends and supporters; and most of all, the members of
NiaOnline. Thank you so much for expressing yourselves.

Some of the contents of this book are adapted from
articles that originally appeared on NiaOnline. We grate-
fully acknowledge the fine work of a number of writers who
have contributed to the site over the years. The titles of
articles from which selected content was adapted for this
book, the dates on which those articles were originally
published, and the writers of the articles are listed below:

"Get Paid What You're Really Worth" parts 1 and 2 (March
5, 2001 and March 19, 2001); "How to Take Advantage of
Mentor Relationships" (May 7, 2001); "Are You the Sole
Sister in the Office?" parts 1 and 2 (October 1, 2001 and
October 15, 2001); "Turn Your Setbacks Into Comebacks,"
parts 1 and 2 (November 5, 2001 and November 19, 2001);
"Network Your Way to Success" (January 7, 2002); "Your
Identity: Keeping It Real on the Job" (February 2, 2002);

"It's Time To Make Over Your Resume" (April 1, 2002); "Are You Selling Yourself Short?" (June 17, 2002); and "Chapter 2 in Your Career" (July 1, 2002) were written for NiaOnline by Carolyn M. Brown.

"For a Better Career in '04, Look to Kwanzaa" (December 8, 2003) and "Celebrating Black History at Work" (February 12, 2004) were written for NiaOnline by Harriette Cole.

SOLE SISTER:
KEEPING YOUR PRIDE
AND SANITY

YOUR IDENTITY
Keeping It Real
on the Job

"We sometimes are schizophrenic, so in the work world you're one thing. At MTV, I had my hair slicked back in a bun and I wore the suit....and then on the weekend my hair went wild and I was two different people. Now it's like, 'No, this is what you get everywhere. This is me.' And so you have to find yourself. You have to know who you are. It goes into personal branding—'What do I want to project?'—and self inquiry — meditation, prayer, journaling, all of that."

Teresa Kay-Aba Kennedy
President of Power Living Enterprises

One of the biggest challenges any black woman faces in corporate America is maintaining her cultural or personal identity while striving to succeed. For example, do you avoid having black artwork or memorabilia (posters, calendars, mugs) displayed in your office or cubicle? Do you shy away from certain types of behaviors, such as talking too long at work with other blacks or eating fried chicken at the company picnic? Do you tend not to socialize with black employees who have a lower rank (say, a receptionist or mail-room clerk), just because it might not look right?

If you answered yes to any of these questions, chances are that you are not keeping it real at work.

It can be challenging to work in the predominantly white corporate world, which talks a good game about cultural diversity as part of corporate policy but may not always follow through with action. Many sisters are especially conflicted because, in addition to feeling forced to decide whether they identify more as black or as American—or whether they should "act" black or white—they are often torn between black and female allegiances.

You may be one of these corporate sisters.

Of course, you may embrace your black identity but choose not to express it at work in the way you adorn your office or how you dress, speak, or wear your hair. It is an issue that often boils down to what makes you—and the white people around you—comfortable.

So just how far should a sister go to tone it down or subjugate her personal identity in order to succeed in the workplace?

Image is everything. But what's appropriate in any given corporate culture is a function of the culture itself: Who sets the policy at the top—someone who is open-minded, or someone who is rigid? What are the rules? What product or service does the company provide, and what image is associated with it?

Whether you're simply striving to fit in or you intend to stay "true to yourself," you have to figure out what will and won't work in your particular environment. These are among the challenges you may face as you move up the corporate ladder:

Your Crowning Glory

Your hairstyle is a part of your cultural expression and your self-expression. The way you wear your hair indeed makes a statement. At a conservative, formal-suit-wearing company, if you were to roll up to the office with dreadlocks, the perception might be that you are more concerned with your own culture than with the corporate culture. At a new high-tech firm that supports innovation, on the other hand, wearing dreadlocks may be considered part of your creativeness.

The beauty of black women is that we can wear a number of different hairstyles: natural, curly, permed, locked, twisted, micro-braided, cornrowed, relaxed, weaved, or wigged. We can sport our natural color or dye our hair blonde, red, or brunette.

"I have run the gamut from having braids to really short cuts to weaves down my back," says Talethea M. Best, CEO and founder of the Best Consulting Group in Voorhees, New Jersey. Over the years she has learned to set boundaries. "When choosing a professional look, I focus first on what is comfortable for me and second on what will be least distracting when I'm working with clients."

Talking The Talk

Another challenge is how we speak. Some black women have voices that tend to be deeper and louder, with more power and resonance, than those of women of other ethnic groups. "I don't go out of my way to monitor my speech. In fact, I speak my mind at work," says Mary Williams, an employee-benefits assistant with Unified Networks, a New Jersey-based accounting firm. "But I always carry myself in a professional manner; that's what matters."

Broken English is one thing; black slang is another. The former should always be left at the door (using proper English is not "talking white"). The latter can occasionally enter, especially once it becomes part of mainstream culture. Still, while "girl, please" and "peep this" are comments you might make to your crew, it would not be wise to introduce your mate to your boss as "your boo"! Nor would any sensible sister be caught dead doing a gooseneck or finger snap at a manager's meeting or client presentation.

Blacks in corporate America have mastered speaking one way at work and another when they are with friends and family. In fact, it is one of our strengths, points out Best, who does interpersonal-skills training for such clients as John Hopkins Healthcare, Oakley Sunglasses, and Prudential.

"People are getting more comfortable speaking the language that is consistent with their audience," she says. "So an African American making a presentation may use different verbal or body language with senior managers than with frontline employees. We are much better at making that adjustment than white people." Bottom line: communicate in whichever manner is most effective for your audience.

Hanging Out Outside Of Work

What if you refuse to socialize with your white coworkers during or after work? What if you socialize only with other black colleagues? You wouldn't want to do anything that might make your white colleagues think you are not a team player, would you? "Sometimes you have to position yourself socially if it is going to be of value to you down the line—say, in helping you get a promotion," Best advises. "You don't want to miss out on things that are relevant to your job that are getting discussed outside of work."

Whether and how you socialize is up to you, but there's no point in trying to be something—or someone—you're not, because people can easily spot a phony. "How well I do my job is what I should be judged on, not who I socialize with or what I wear," says Williams, noting that she has gone to dinner and happy hour with white and black colleagues alike. She adds that she doesn't hide her spiritual side. "I have different inspirational sayings, such as 'Too blessed to be stressed,' hanging in my office. I listen to my gospel music in the background."

Labels are a part of life. We are constantly confronted by people who want to categorize us and who expect us to act and look a certain way. At the same time, society's images and expectations do change. Today a sister can practically shave her head and not be questioned about her sexuality, as opposed to the situation just five years ago. "There is enough flexibility in this corporate image to be you," says Best. Ultimately, you must define yourself by your own standards.

2

ARE YOU THE
Sole Sister
in the Office?

"I think too often women of color underestimate and are unprepared for the challenges that they face as they go into corporate environments, other high-pressured environments, or their own businesses. They believe that because they are talented and smart and have been successful in the past, it's automatic entrée to success in the future. In reality it is just a precursor, which just sort of gets you in the door. It's a cost of entry, but it's no guarantee for success."

Paula Sneed
Group Vice President of Kraft Foods

Andrea graduated from college armed with a freshly minted degree and ready to show off her marketing skills. She landed a job as a public relations assistant for an import company.

But as the only African American in her department, Andrea feels her ideas are often dismissed.

Recently the company was trying to break into the urban market. Her superiors asked her if they should have rappers sing about a certain vodka. Because it was a very upscale product, she suggested they market to black executives. But her superiors didn't think that would be a stable market.

People are constantly telling twenty-three-year-old Andrea that she has to pay her dues. "But I don't think I should have to sell myself short," says the young entrepreneur, who co-founded a promotions and events-planning firm with some college chums. Andrea says her supervisors are nice people, but they don't understand her need to be challenged. "The work I am doing is brainless work," says Andrea. "It is stressful mentally. I wake up not wanting to go to work."

Does this sound familiar? It doesn't matter if you are at the top or just starting out in corporate America—being the only sister in the office can be a laborious experience. Deborah A. Watts, management consultant and author of *101 Ways to Know You're "Black" in Corporate America* (Watts-Five Productions, 1998), has written about the realities of being the only one. Here, Watts identifies the most common issues that sisters face in corporate America:

Do we still need affirmative action?

Yes The playing field isn't level.
246 (82%)

No It's reverse discrimination.
19 (6%)

I'm not sure
35 (12%)

Results of a July 2004 online poll of 300 members of NiaOnline's Consumer Advisory Panel. All respondents were black women eighteen and over.

1. **You lack support.** A number of sisters don't have a support system in the office or a mentor, someone who can provide career guidance and serve as a sounding board for problems.

2. **You don't have a career plan.** Too often, sisters fail to establish criteria for success. They don't map out where they want to be in one year, five years, or even ten years—let alone what steps they need to take to get there.

3. **You fail to take control of your career.** There is a tendency to play the victim: "My boss wouldn't let me!" You may have a well-thought-out plan, but if you wait for others to act on it, you may never get anywhere.

4. **You are left out of the game.** Being the lone sister often means you are excluded from opportunities to develop solid relationships with the higher-ups in the company or key clients. You tend to shy away from immersing yourself in the corporate culture.

5. **You are not taken seriously.** Being the only black woman also often means that you are ignored. Your input may not be viewed as something that is valuable and viable. You may find that you have to repeat yourself or prove yourself over and over again.

6. **You are stereotyped.** Misperceptions abound in the corporate workplace. Speak your mind, and you are seen as a black woman with an attitude. Disagree, and you are seen as not being a team player. Ask for what you want, and you are considered pushy.

The key to working in corporate America is to understand that it is a game, points out Watts: "The problem with many African Americans is that oftentimes we walk into the business arena suited up to play football, when the actual game being played is baseball." Your reaction may be, "I am not prepared to play baseball. I have studied and worked really hard to play football." And so you spend years waiting for the game to change. But the game is typically the same from company to company, Watts adds. The reality of the situation is that you have two choices. You can either say: "Let me figure out this game and the rules. Once I get it, I plan to play to win!" Or you can make this statement your own: "This isn't my game. I am going to find me a football field." (Most folks who say this are entrepreneurs.)

Do you have a mentor?

Yes	68 (23%)
No	177 (59%)
Not now, but I did in the past.	55 (18%)

Results of a July 2004 online poll of 300 members of NiaOnline's Consumer Advisory Panel. All respondents were black women eighteen and over.

Whether you find yourself the only sister in the office because you live in an area where there are few blacks or because you're a pioneer in your industry or company, you face similar challenges.

Watts identifies these strategies for combating the challenges of being the single black female—and even making the situation work in your favor.

1. **Find a mentor.** This doesn't have to be someone who likes you—or who even works within the company. The idea is to find someone who is well respected and has access to power. You have to see yourself as a valuable commodity to the company and your mentor. Take the power approach and say to that person, "Here is what I can offer you." You want someone who will be interested in partnering with you in your success.

2. **Integrate life and career goals.** Your game plan has to include your personal, career, and civic goals. Often something will occur in your personal life that will have an impact on your career, such as the decision to have a

baby. You need to be able to plan for how this will affect your career and your life. Have you made yourself valuable enough to the company that your boss would be willing to work "with you and not against you"? Learn how to build strong relationships within the company, and you can work just about any career or life plan you want.

3. **Take responsibility for your own success.** As black women, we are often spectators of our own demise. We may not be aggressive enough or feel sufficiently confident to ask for what we want. And then, when some of us do ask, we get turned down—maybe because our skills are legitimately questioned, or maybe purely because of racism. You need to have a good understanding of your strengths and weaknesses and then find ways to fill in the gaps. Use whatever tools are at your disposal, including a career counselor and online career-assessment tests.

4. **Bring added value to the table.** Being heard for the sake of being noticed isn't going to cut it. Don't just identify a problem—offer a solution. Tell your boss what you are capable of doing, but make sure you back up your statements with performance. You need to market yourself to your peers, your boss, and your superior's boss. Realize that this is an ongoing process. Another part of the game is making your boss and your company look good. You may not get direct recognition in such instances, but that is part of being a team player.

5. **Demystify yourself.** Get to know the boss. White people tend to think that black women don't want anyone in their "personal business." This is often held against us. One way to combat this and other misperceptions is to

give your superiors strategic bits of personal information to diminish your mystique. You will soon find yourself part of the mix, which will put you in a prime position to observe who are the real players.

"Shattering *the* Glass Ceiling"

NIA ENTERPRISES LEADERSHIP SUMMIT,
NEW YORK, APRIL 30, 2004

"I became part of IBM and said, 'Let me try to shatter this concrete ceiling and move my way up.' But [it did not happen] fast enough ... I think they say that the bumblebee should not be able to fly, because aerodynamically the wings are too light to hold the body. So 'impossible,' to me, is not a fact, it's an opinion. So I said, 'I've got to find a way to even go higher and higher.'"

Daphne Jones
Executive Director of Information Management
for Johnson & Johnson

Nia Enterprises' popular Leadership Summits give black women from all walks of life the opportunity to get together to share ideas about success and fulfillment at work and at home. Summit participants include leading black women from business and civic life and speakers have been a who's who of some of the most successful women in the country, including former presidential candidate and U.S. Ambassador Carol Moseley Braun, poet Nikki Giovanni, BET president Debra Lee, CNBC CEO and president Pamela Thomas-Graham, Magna Securities CEO Patricia Winans, and SoftSheen-Carson's president Candace Matthews, among a host of other notables.

2004 was a breakthrough year for Nia Enterprises. Enthusiastic responses to our Leadership Summits compelled us to hold two: one in New York City in April, and a Chicago summit in June. We decided to record various sessions of the New York summit and include the transcripts in this Nia Guide to make some of the dynamic exchange and lessons taught and learned available to you.

Cheryl Mayberry McKissack, CEO Of Nia Enterprises: Today you're going to hear advice from some of Wall Street's leading women, and a top executive in corporate America. And they're going to talk about how you can shape your career, gain power, and still enjoy what truly matters. We're excited to present to you these very special ladies who will share their wisdom on this topic.

Our speakers include Daphne Jones, who is executive director of information management for Johnson & Johnson, and Patricia Winans, who is CEO of Magna Securities Corporation and was recently on the cover of *Fortune* magazine. In a news-style interview, both Patricia, who's one of the top black women entrepreneurs on Wall Street, and Daphne, who is a leading black female executive at a Fortune 500 company, will discuss the following: How you can win at the career game without losing yourself, identify mentors, protégées and allies who will support your career, and manage being the sole—S.O.L.E.—sister in the office.

NiaOnline: Daphne Jones is the executive director of information management for Johnson & Johnson. She oversees Johnson & Johnson's information technology operations. Pat Winans owns Magna Securities, a Wall Street securities firm. She started Magna in 1993 after she saw an opportunity and followed her instincts.

One of the interesting things about Daphne and Pat is that they both showed an early determination to succeed. Daphne finished both her BA and her MBA in four years—that's a phenomenal feat. Pat started bond trading at the age of twenty, before she even graduated from school. So you can see that both these women started very early. And you can see their determination.

Let's start with Pat. You started working in finance at twenty. How hard was it to get into that business? Into Wall Street, which is traditionally seen as an enclave of white men?

Patricia Winans: I have to be honest and say I fell into it by accident. I started working at the First National Bank of Chicago when, I guess, I was eighteen years old. I was a bank teller, and back in those days we would all get together on a Thursday night and go out for drinks and, you know, style and profile and do all that. And there were all these people who were all that.

So we were out and I finally had a few drinks and had the courage to say, "You know, I'm a teller but I really would like to make more money." I guess I was making maybe $8,000 a year at the time. And I said, "What department in the bank pays the most money?" I really wanted to know. And they said, "Well, you've got to go to the bond department for that." And I said, "What are bonds?" They're like, "You know, stocks and bonds." "No, I don't know stocks and bonds. My family didn't have any of that."

But lo and behold, about a couple of months later there was a job on the bulletin board and it said, "In the bond department," and it was for a receptionist. I thought, wow, I can do that, you know. So I did that. And I didn't get that particular job because I was really over-qualified, having been a teller, but the value of having been a bank teller really taught me my math skills, because when you're a bank teller one of the things that you have to do at the end of every day is balance your cash drawer. And if you balance to the penny, they say you pop. And you get a pat on the back. And that's how you get to management if you want to remain a bank teller.

So, eventually I got this job in the bond department, the next time it came up, because I went to that first interview. They remembered me when another position became open. One of the reasons they hired me was because I had very good command of English. I could talk fast, because it's a very fast-paced market. You've got to be able to relay the information, it has to be clear. And I didn't know this at the time but I did have a knack for math, having been a bank teller. Then when I became involved in this job as a sales assistant, I went back to night school. And I started studying finance and economics and all that I was learning about economics I was able to apply to the real world.

So, while I sort of fell into it, once I was in the position, there was an incidcnt that opened my eyes even wider, and I began to understand why people said it's the division that pays the most. As a sale assistant in that job, one of the things I had to do was the monthly reports where I would calculate everybody's commission. And having been a bank teller, I was good at that. So, I could see how much money everyone on that trading desk made because they got a percentage of what they sold. They were making anywhere between $300,000, $400,000 a year, which to me at the time sounded like an awful lot of money because I was making maybe $12,000 a year as a sales assistant on the trading desk.

And because I was so eager to help everybody, when people would travel they would have me cover their book and talk to their clients. So one day—I'll never forget the guy—one of them said, "Pat, I'm going to be on the road and I want you to cover my book. If we get these type of bonds, you call one of these types of accounts. If we get this, you call that." And actually one of [the Leadership Summit] sponsors, Northern Trust, they had a bank department and they bought bonds that were always selling very close to a hundred cents on the dollar. We call them par bonds. And I called up because this big offering went on the board, and what they wanted were bonds that were priced close to a hundred and that had very high-quality ratings. So a state of Maryland, AAA-rated, five-percent coupon due 2015 went on the board and I thought, "Hmm, he told me to call Northern Trust if we got something like that." I called Northern Trust, they bought those bonds right on the phone. That was a $20 million block. And I didn't know what to do. [Laughter]

I was like, ah, OK…hold on. So I said, well, just mimic everybody else. Stood up, put my hand on my hip, called the head trader. "Ah, ah, selling 20 million, State of Maryland, five due 2015 at list"—meaning at the price you have them listed. And the trader was like, "To who?" I'm like, "Northern Trust." He says, "Done!" And everybody was like high-fiving me and I'm like—you know . . . [Laughter]

Got back on the phone, "OK, I am selling you 20 million State of Maryland, five," and I'm doing this bond calculation, giving them the exact dollar price. And I hang up the phone and everybody was like, "Oh, my God, who was that? Who was that?" And so everybody wanted me to cover their account when they were traveling. And I figured out why—that month when I did the monthly report the commission that the broker got on that trade was $40,000. And here I was still making $12,000. [Laughter]

So I went to my sales manager and I said, "I want to be in sales. How can I be in sales?" And he said, "Well, first of all, you're not old enough. You don't have a college degree, you don't read *The Wall Street Journal.* You don't do this, you don't do that." And I said, "Well, I'm going to do it. And when I do it I want to be in sales." And he said, "But you're not old enough. The people that you're going to be talking to, these portfolio managers, they have this, they have that." And you know, I said, "But I can do it. I did it already."

And so I was lucky because I got to do a lot of it before it was really my time to do it. And it just went from there. I wanted to be on commission. You know, sometimes when people tell you, you know, that job only pays commission, take a second look, because you're betting on yourself and if you know what you can do, then you're better off with that upside opportunity. I couldn't wait to be on commission. And before really getting into my own company, because I know that was just one question, I never had a job that paid me a salary after that until I started my own company.

So I was on commission my whole life. I'm still on commission, it's just that my commission pays all my staff people and I have maybe twenty people who are on commission who work for me now.

NiaOnline: That leads us to other ways we can shatter the glass ceiling. Because you took the information you learned at a young age and used it to advance and then moved on. Let's get into that again a little bit later. For now, let's get to Daphne's story. It's an interesting one as well. Daphne took a different route. After she graduated from school, she went on to IBM, where she worked for fourteen years before moving on. Daphne, how do you shatter the glass ceiling at a place like IBM, which embodies, to a lot of people, corporate America? You started there at a young age.

Daphne Jones: Right, right. You're talking about going in by chance and I kind of made a choice. When I was in college, I wanted to work for IBM. But even before that—you talked about trying to shatter preconceived notions. When I was in high school I had a counselor who said to me that I would never be anything more than a secretary.

So, he said, "Take some typing classes, get some shorthand under your belt." It was a time when nursing was a big profession and [being a] secretary was a big profession and education was also large as well. And he said, "Take some classes." So I did that and got a scholarship for secretarial school and did that for a while.

I was secretary at *Woman's Day* magazine in Chicago. And a situation came when the editor was dictating something to me and he used the word I thought was "copulation" and what he said was, "compilation." So I'm typing this letter up and he said, "Daphne, this is not correct." And I said, "What am I doing here?" There was an epiphany that came to me that instead of me taking orders from someone, I should be giving orders. So I decided at that point to go to college. I went to Illinois State University and said, "I'm just going to zoom my way through as quickly as I can, and pledge a sorority and all that." I decided that by choice, I wanted to work for IBM.

You talk about a glass ceiling. A glass ceiling implies that you can see what's happening up above you, that there's some rows above you. I'm telling you, for African American women, or for women in general, there's a concrete ceiling that's really above us that you have to find a way to chisel your way through and pop your head up there so you can make sure that you are part of what's happening in the future. So I became part of IBM and said to myself, let me try to shatter this concrete ceiling and move my way up. But not fast enough as I wanted to do. I ended up, actually, being an engineer, and then I became an instructor and I became a manager.

I think they say that the bumblebee should not be able to fly because aerodynamically the wings are too light to hold the body. So, impossible to me is not a fact, it's an opinion. So I said, I've got to find a way to even go higher and higher. I was able to leave IBM after fifteen years or so and then I went on to my current employer, Johnson & Johnson. I started to shatter the concrete-glass ceiling, if you will, by saying in my mind, what is it that I'm here to do? And what is it that I can do? And nobody ever said it was going to be easy—and nobody was right! It wasn't easy going there, but there are ways through mentors, through planning your plan and having role models that are in front of you who you can kind of mimic. And either through talking with them or seeing them from afar, be able to mimic some of the things that they do.

NiaOnline: Daphne has pointed out before that oftentimes we African American women in corporate America are given responsibilities and take on jobs but are not given the title that goes with those responsibilities. Daphne, could you address how you deal with that? How do you go in and say that your title should be in line with your responsibilities? Of course, you know there's going to be pushback to that kind of request, but how did you deal with that?

Daphne Jones: Well, you talk about purpose. You have to first have a goal in mind, an unwavering goal. You first have to say, "What's your destination?" As Steven Covey says, "Begin with the end in mind." So that's what you first have to do. And then you're working with different tools in your toolkit. One of those is mentoring. I mean, I believe strongly in having a champion, a sponsor, a coach, a mentor, someone from whom you can learn the rules of engagement, learn the rules of the game. So that was one thing that I had to do.

The second thing was you have to deliver. You know, Austin Powers talks about, "Baby, it's about the business, Baby." It's about delivering on time, early, flawlessly, all the time. Because without performance, your personality—you know, your polish—all those things don't really matter. So you have to be able to say, "Here's what I've done. I've delivered."

So you come to a point where you're doing this job so well, and then you have to keep on going to that next step, ask for maybe not the promotion, but ask for stretch assignments where you're given more authority. As I was saying before, there are times when you look for the responsibility and you get all these people, you get all this stuff, and you're promised an opportunity to have authority. Get the authority. And then get the people that you can give the responsibility to.

So you really have to start with delivering on time, whatever your goal is, whatever you're there to do from a business perspective, and then your mentors can do more than just be role models—they can open doors for you. They can shine a spotlight onto you. They say that when you first join a company, the mentors kind of show you the way. They're like a flashlight and they guide you and say, "Walk here, walk here," and "This is how you direct, this is how you behave."

But when you go into senior management, the mentor shines the spotlight onto you. So that's how you're able to get that authority and get that position that you really desire. It's by having a mentor who helps to shine that light on you. But you've got to deliver as well.

NiaOnline: Let's talk more about that in a bit. Pat has said that she didn't have mentors. Pat, how did you advance in your career without any mentors? Were you just simply aggressive? How did you see *through* the concrete, as Daphne put it?

Patricia Winans: For me it was a matter of pride in that I was afraid to let anyone know that I wasn't good enough to make it. I have peers on Wall Street and we all sort of know each other. People tend to know when you get hired by somebody, and people tend to know when you botch up an account. And this is reflected today in the culture of my company. I wanted everything to be done perfectly, so it was just a matter of pride that if someone was going to trust me to handle their account, I really knew what the service was that I needed to deliver.

And at that point in my business, you go through four major points, which maybe we'll have a chance to talk about later, as you go from being an entrepreneur to a CEO. At each point in those businesses you do things that are different. When you first start your company, you're the doer. You do everything that has to be done because it's maybe you and maybe one other person.

And then as you begin to bring on a little bit of cash flow, you bring in these other people to circle you and surround you and help you and you become the dele-gater. So the challenge at that point was to make all these people to whom I was delegating my responsibility understand how critically important it was to do it and to do it right. Because it's so competitive on Wall Street—the money. You screw up, you get fired.

I mean, in corporate America, you know, you get hired and you have to keep your job. As an entrepreneur who is providing services to corporate America, the moment you do something wrong on that account, they call you and tell you that your responsibility to them has been terminated effective thirty days or immediately. And so you've lost that account. So, for me it's all about getting hired over and over and over, because every time I get hired by a new client, the revenue goes up.

I have to rely on my references from an account that I did a good job on to help me get hired in that next job. So if I don't do a good job in the first situation, then I don't continue to get hired and my company folds and goes away. So it was really just a matter of pride, getting it done right so that people could say good things about me.

NiaOnline: Did anybody give you advice? Did anybody tell you what to focus on and what not to focus on? And how did you make the decision to go out on your own?

Patricia Winans: Well, people were—OK, it's a two-part question. First, what did people do to sort of mold me? I guess that was the culture that I started out with initially, because there's big money involved, and there had to be accuracy in every single transaction.

So people would always pull me aside, you know, when I—back in those days, it's funny that I find myself saying this like your grandparents would say to you, "Back in those days we didn't have this." But really, when I was an assistant on the trading desk, we didn't have personal computers. We barely had a mainframe. When I used to do that report, I had to draw the report on a sheet of paper and actually put in the numbers. And the first time I got a number wrong, I was ripped to shreds by my sales manager. And I said, "That'll never happen again." Because that number being wrong resulted in someone getting the wrong commission on a trade. And I knew that couldn't happen. So it was just implanted in my mind, you know, you have to be perfect all the time. You're dealing with people's money. Whether it's a commission or whether it's a client's money.

So that was so ingrained, and it wasn't that people sat me down and said it had to be done this way, it was just, this is the way it's going to be done and this is the way you have to do it. And now, I have that same attitude in my own company because certain things have to be done according to regulations and then, when you get beyond that, you have performance and values, in terms of what you look for in your employees.

But when I started my own company—to get to the second part of the question—I was thirty-two years old and I guess I was just very idealistic. I never thought that I would start my own company, but I had had—and I'll share some really personal things with you—I had had a major surgery because I had fibroids in my uterus that needed to be removed. And once I had that surgery, it was a six-week recovery and one of the things that I had to do was go out for a walk around the block every single day, as part of the recovery process.

So I would get up early in the morning—I was used to getting up early anyway, I had to be at the trading desk at 7 a.m. every morning, which meant getting up at 5:30. So I decided I would get up and do my walk early because not that many people were on the street. I was living right here in Manhattan on 45th between 1st and 2nd.

And all I had to do was circle that block. But that was a hard walk for me to make, and I had to walk very slowly. Well, for the very, very first time, in doing that walk, I saw homeless people. And I thought, why are all these homeless people sleeping in these doorways and these cubbies and I never noticed them before? Maybe because I was just moving too fast.

But it occurred to me that here I was in the situation I was in because I had this problem with my uterus. I mean, if you've ever experienced any of this—us as black women—you know that it's torture. But if I hadn't had insurance, I would have died because I literally would have bled to death. OK, and when I saw this black woman who was homeless, I said, "Oh my God, she doesn't have insurance. You know, what's going to become of all these people?"

So I was aware of what Muriel Siebert was doing. She was going to people that could give her business saying, "If you do business with me, we'll give fifty percent of the profit back to charity." And I thought, "I've got to do something about all these people on the street. I've got to, you know, get some way where there's all this money on Wall Street and funnel some of it back into these homeless shelters."

And I was watching all this television during my recovery, and Tony Johnson came on one evening and he talked about taking control of your life. When I recovered from my surgery, two weeks later I went back in and I resigned. People said, "What are you going to do?" I said, "I'm going to start my own company, and I'm going to get managers to do business with me and I'm going to give money back to homeless shelters."

And it was a great idea at the time. Didn't work. But because I was willing to do it, and had started doing it, this reporter heard about it, wrote a little piece on it in *The Wall Street Journal*, and a consultant in Atlanta called me up and said, "I understand you do commission recapture." And I said, "No, I never heard of it before, what is it?" And he said, "Well, it's sort of like what you do with your charities, people give you business and you give fifty percent of the money back." And he said, "But instead of giving it to charity, you give it back to the pension fund."

There's a whole reason why this exists on Wall Street and it's far too long a story for me to go into right now. But I said, "Hmm, sounds like the math is all the same. I know how to do the reporting." He said, "Well, I'm going to send you an RFP." And I said, "OK, but what's an RFP?" [Laughter] And he said, "Well, it's just this form you fill out and you send it back to me." And I said, "OK." So I sent it back and all these managers that I'd been trying to get to allow my firm to execute these transactions for them so I'd make the commission and donate this money back, said "You know, this doesn't really add value. Giving money back to charity doesn't really help me decide what I'm going to buy and sell. It doesn't add value to our clients."

Well, when I got this RFP, and letters went to certain managers to do business with my company, it was like the floodgates opened. And all these commissions just started streaming in and I said, "Well, I think I need to do commission recapture." So today I probably have just under fifty contracts, and that was the initial growth of my business, where I ramped up all these contracts because I focused in on a niche as a minority firm and was really one of the only minority firms who was doing it at the time.

And when that consultant called me, he called me because he wanted some minority participation for the client who wanted to do this type of service. He couldn't find one single firm on the Street that was minority owned and I was the closest thing to it because I was doing my philanthropic product called From Wall Street to Your Street. But it was the same mechanism. So being philanthropic and wanting to share and give back was what got me in the game and then I was able to identify my niche, because, again, that came to me.

NiaOnline: We'll answer questions soon but here's one thing for Daphne before we move on. Daphne, you're very passionate about mentoring. You've said that you don't see many managers at Johnson & Johnson like yourself. So your mentors are people who don't look like you. Can you say more about that? Then we'll go to questions from the audience.

Daphne Jones: Sure. There are some African American vice presidents and executive directors, et cetera, at Johnson & Johnson. The challenge is that, as you get closer to the top, there aren't as many as there should be. So you have a whole slew of African American women and men who are at the lower levels of the organization who are clamoring for those three or four or five vice presidents who are just so very, very busy.

So you know there's a saying that goes, "Why did Jesse James rob banks? Because that's where the money is." So where do you go for expert advice and support? You go to the folks who pretty much built the industry, and who industry is still somewhat more geared to, and that's a lot of times white men. And there's white women, and then there's African American women, and somewhere lost in there is African American males. So there are mentors that I have who don't look like me.

You don't have to have only one mentor, they don't have to only look like you. They don't have to be your same gender, they don't have to be in your same functional area or even your same company. You can get mentors based on what your need is. It all starts with purpose—what's your goal, what's your vision? Based on whatever that is, you can have a mentor or two or three or four, and based on that person your conversation changes according to what you're trying to get out of that individual.

So I would have an African American male who's a mentor, a white female—there are two white females and a white male who still mentor me. And based on what I want to talk about, those are some of the things that happen. So, again, they shine a light, they help, they open doors, they're advocates, they challenge, they say, "This is something that I would have done differently, a little bit differently, Daphne." So there are ways that you can get that kind of support through all levels of the organization. But you first have to say in your mind, "I don't have to have an African American female." It helps, but you don't have to have that.

NiaOnline: We'll answer questions now.

Summit Delegate: I'm a teacher in the public schools here in New York. And I was overjoyed to hear both of you speak about the importance of education. The problem with our youngsters today is that they feel they have nothing to look forward to. And it was interesting to see how without a real goal, and then having some time in the world of work, you came upon a goal.

These youngsters today don't come into high school with a goal. My question is how can we challenge the youngsters to develop a feeling or a pride about being someone early, such as at the elementary level?

Daphne Jones: Well, I have a sixteen-year-old son. And it's funny, he hasn't got the best discipline that I'd like to see him have. You know, as a hard-charging mom you want your boy on point all the time. And he's not there. But there are groups that have what I call the pre-college initiative kind of support. If you go to—and I'm just going to name one or a couple—NSBE, the society for black engineers, and there's the black MBAs—they have programs that really get girls and boys involved in understanding what they can be.

My son wants to be an architect, but he has to get more A's than he already has. But he's going into that knowing what he wants to do. There are groups that are black-owned or black-oriented that will help a child get exposure to certain areas. So NSBE, the black engineers' society, has architects, engineers, technology folks. And I did an event there about a month or so ago. There were a thousand kids in the room, and a lot of them were girls and boys but they were from seventh grade to high school seniors. That's what they call their pre-college initiative.

These kids will go on and they now have purpose, they have a plan, they have an idea that what they can become does exist. And they don't have to be a rap star only or someone who is just doing whatever they do that doesn't have to do with education. So I think there are avenues that we can take as teachers, parents, aunts, uncles—you know, introduce some of those kids to those environments that do support pre-college kinds of thinking.

A lot of women, a lot of girls steer away from technical fields. And you can take a Myers-Briggs test—if anyone hasn't heard of it, Myers-Briggs, you can get it online. You can actually take a girl or a boy and say, "Take this test. It's a test about preferences: what do you prefer?" And based on what comes out of that, you're opened up to whether you could be a lawyer, you could be a judge, you could be a marketing analyst. It's like twenty questions, really simple. And at the end of it, it says these are some of the careers that you can have. So there're different avenues, I think, that you could take as a teacher, parent, aunt, uncle, whatever to get them engaged that way.

Patricia Winans: Did you want me to respond as well? Just to your point of how do you get them to have that pride—I think you really do have to put role models in front of them who make a true connection. In my own family, because my mom died when I was young, you know, I had three sisters—I was the fourth—who all had children out of wedlock. So when you talk about this inner-city phenomenon, it's not so far removed from many of our own families.

I have seven nephews, five of whom have felony records, have been behind bars, have been in gangs, have dealt drugs. And it was a really tough battle for me to get them out of that mentality. The way I was able to do

it was just by showing them and helping them to understand what it means to have success and all that success
can bring. Because so many of them have been in generation after generation where there was no real success,
that they can't see it, they can't conceptualize it.

Then to get them to understand how to achieve it,
people ask me all the time, "How did you become such a
big success?" I made it because I focused on the activity.
It's not the goal that's going to get you there, it's the
activity to reach that goal. My nephews are now working
and going back to school and want to become entrepreneurs because they have seen firsthand what my success
has done for my entire family. So they have to hear the
stories and the person giving that story has to really be
able to connect. And I think I made the connection
because I was one of them. I was from the ghetto. I did it,
you know. I took them out of the ghetto and now they're
doing it.

Annette Chow: Hi, my name is Annette Chow from Multi-
cultural Marketing Resources. And I just want to let you
know, one of my clients is the Grant Foundation and they
just signed a deal with Tyco. So if anybody has kids that are
looking for grants, they have a three-year contract with
them and it just happened in the last week or so. So if
anybody's interested, let me know and I can forward that
information on to you. So they're looking for minority
kids, mainly African American and Hispanic.

Daphne Jones: Great, let me add a point to that. At Johnson
& Johnson there's a group called the African American
Leadership Council and they're a bunch of African

Americans, vice president on down, that are working to increase the diversity, you know, mix, if you will, at Johnson & Johnson at all levels in the company. So we got an email about three weeks ago about the number of grants and scholarships that are available to African American kids, teenagers if you will, who want to go to college, that are turned back or that are not ever tapped because people don't know that this money is out there. You know, UNCF, some of the obvious ones, Rhodes Scholar, Coca-Cola, Tyco, a ton of them. And if anyone's interested, I can give that to the folks here.

But do not let an opportunity go by. Again, Jesse James robbed banks because that's where the money is. We've got to go where the money is and not be complacent, not just sit back and hope that something will happen. We have to go out and get what we want as opposed to waiting for it to come to us. I just wanted to add that point.

Summit Delegate: Good morning, I work for an investment magazine, on the business side. I'm really intrigued by the dynamics of identifying and developing a mentorship relationship. I kind of fell into this business. I used to work in investment management. And I'm not necessarily looking for a mentor who looks just like me because, in the upper echelons of the magazine publishing business everybody is at two companies, *Essence* and *Black Enterprise.*

I'm interested to hear your insights or just some hints and key ideas as to how to approach someone. I mean, you don't want to make it sound like a job interview. It's not. You're looking for someone to help you along the way. And I'm interested in both of your insights on that.

33

Patricia Winans: Well, with me some of the younger people that I mentor now—because my schedule takes me on the road like ninety percent of the time, I live out of a suitcase, My shoes are all scuffed and my nails are not done because I don't have time in New York—but a lot of it's done via email. The way I keep in touch with my office now, and the younger people in my office, we have all of these conversations that are going back and forth. And my blackberry is like my source for everything.

So sometimes there will be times when I can sit down with someone personally, but I feel like I have fifteen conversations going at all times because of people that I talk to and people that I mentor. And sometimes it's just that little email that comes in, that somebody needs to tap you on that. While I'm drying my hair, I'm answering my emails no matter where I am in the country.

So I think if you can make your feelings known, people are really, really open. It amazes me how much I say yes. And I get so many requests that sometimes I have to say no, because it's a matter of time. But if I can help someone and I can do it in a way that works for me and my schedule, I'll do that. And for me it's that email dialogue that works. So, you just have to tell someone you need them, because I think that that—it makes me feel good when someone says they need me, more so than when they say, "I want you to do this for me."

Daphne Jones: Let me also address that question because, you know, you talk about the approach. I've been asked that question quite a few times. If you are in a place where you see someone who really catches you because they embody what you call success, and the organization says that they're also successful and so they're obviously on a track going forward, what I usually do is I find a way to first meet them. Sometimes folks don't always want you just to say, "Will you mentor me?" you know. They like the roundabout approach, right?

So what I would usually suggest to folks is, do it on the down-low. Well, maybe that's a bad term—[Laughter] — but I do it in a discreet way, is that OK? You ask them, you say, "I've got a question I'd love to ask you. I've got a challenging opportunity, I would love to just bounce some ideas off of you. Can we do lunch?" And schedule that lunch a month from now so it's not like tomorrow or in the next hour and a half. But schedule some time and then you really need to have a discussion, a problem that you want them to try to help you solve.

Next thing you know, at the end of that conversation, the end of that lunch, the end of that dinner, whatever it is, you say, "You know what, this was really great. Do you mind if I just call you every once in a while just to bounce some additional ideas off of you? You are amazing." You know, you kind of butter them up a little bit. And they will not say no.

To Pat's point, you know, when you arrive in an organization, you want to get as much help as you can get. But as you reach a certain level, you really want to do that push-pull technique, where you push forward but you pull somebody along with you as you're going. So it would be very rare that you'll find someone that says no, I will not have lunch with you. But then, sooner or later, as you meet with them the second or third or fourth time, then you say, "Well, you know, this is great. I have a couple of goals

I'd love to share with you." And you kind of ease into it like you do with a dating relationship or whatever. You kind of walk into it a little slowly and do it a discreet level.

NiaOnline: We have one more question and then we have to wrap this session up.

Summit Delegate: Hi. It's been a very interesting discussion this morning. We've talked about the struggles and challenges that the ladies have been through. I was wondering if you can share what's been the most fulfilling aspect of your career?

Patricia Winans: For me every year has been totally different and my career has been a career, as an entrepreneur. But I think getting through last year was the most fulfilling, probably. And if you ask me a year from now, I probably would have a different story. But last year was particularly challenging because Wall Street was going through so much turmoil. My revenues were down; my lease in my old space was up. I had to expand, I wanted to diversify my revenue stream. So, just being able to walk in my office now, which is a brand-new office—well, I've been there for nine months now—that was really big for me. To have a reception area that has marble on the floor, and have it feel like Goldman Sachs. I mean, it's like you arrived.

So, in spite of all the business and everything else I've done, just pulling it all together under one roof in a major way has been—I mean, sometimes I just have to still ask myself if I'm dreaming. So that's been the highlight at this point, my new office facility, because it's personal to me, because everything in there is something that I labored for. And that was just a real highlight for me.

I've had really big contracts. My clients consist of people like Boeing, Lockheed Martin, Disney, Semper Energy, SBC Communications, Calpers, Calsters, City of Seattle, City of Philadelphia, City of Atlanta, and a whole host of other clients. And that was all great bringing in those contracts. But just knowing that I could pull it all together under one roof the way I did last year at a time when my revenues were down, at a time when everyone was saying, "You can't expand. The economy's bad." I'm like, "Well, I can get this rent now for twelve dollars cheaper a square foot than I could have got it two years ago." And no one believed in it. And I made the decision and I did it. And I'm so glad that I did because now it's a new year and Wall Street's doing good again. [Applause] Thank you, that was my highlight.

NiaOnline: We'll let Daphne answer that and then wrap things up.

Daphne Jones: OK, it's funny, the fulfilling part about my career is just realizing that my career is not a full-time job, it's my life that's my full-time job. And part of my giving to the organizations—sure we do technology, sure we develop all these systems that help companies and help Johnson & Johnson out. But I think the biggest impact for me has been my ability to help generate some energy around diversity at Johnson & Johnson. And part of what I really look forward to all the time is being able to have other African American women and women of color—because I'm not only focusing on African American women, although that's a big part of my focus—is to develop the leadership that comes with that.

At the end of the day, I don't want to be the sole sister in a room. I want to be able to look behind me and say that there were a lot more African American women because of what I did at the ALC level—the African American Leadership Council—at Johnson & Johnson, that now the African American women are more and more populated within the company at higher levels. So that to me is what has made the difference. In the last two years I've been very heavily involved with that and that was more important and more fulfilling for me than building a computer system. [Applause]

Cheryl McKissack I want to tell you just a couple of quick stories. You talked about networking and mentors. This morning, I met these women for the first time. So these are all my sisters, but I did not know them previously. And I will tell you, Patricia, I met her on the cover of *Fortune* magazine, that's how I met her. I saw her on the cover and I picked up the magazine and I put it back for a moment because I saw this black woman on the cover. And I said, who is that? And I said, I'm going to find out who she is.

So I searched her down. She travels all the time and I didn't have any luck getting in touch with her. But my husband's in the investment business and I said to me, "You've got to know this woman." I mean, he's married to me but he's not dead, so I figured, she's gorgeous, she works in the field—[Laughter]. He's got to know her! And he said, "I don't know her, but I think I know some-body who does." And a guy that works for him who was from New York knew her. But we still hadn't gotten to her. He knew of her but didn't know her.

Finally after a couple of dealings, I found a friend, a very good friend of hers who also knew this gentleman that my husband knew, and that's how we got to Patricia. And as you can imagine, she is traveling all the time, very, very busy, and took time to come out to speak to all of us this morning, so I really want to thank her for that, because she didn't have to do that.

Patricia Winans: You're very welcome, I'm glad to be here.

Cheryl McKissack Daphne has an interesting story too. Daphne got up at 4:00 a.m. to be here, because she lives in Princeton. So, you can imagine, that takes about two hours, I hear, on a good day. Daphne was recommended by a very high-ranking executive, one of the top African American women executives in the country, and she said, "I've got the person that you should ask." And so I called her. It was a cold call. And she didn't hang up on me. [Laughter] And that's how we got her here.

So, you know, believe me, even though I really do have the pleasure of meeting all of these wonderful black women, I don't know all of them. I mean, we do have a half-degree of separation. You just have to figure out a way to get to them so that you can have them come here and share it.

TAKE NOTE:

How Will You Shatter The Glass Ceiling?

How will you shatter the glass ceiling in your career? As you plan your breakthrough, take a few moments to answer the following questions raised by Daphne Jones and Patricia Winans, using the notes section below:

1. What are three things that I must do to reach my career goals?

2. Are there any "stretch" assignments I can take to show that I can handle more authority?

3. Who are the individuals who could mentor me in my career, and how will I approach them?

_____

_____

_____

_____

_____

_____

_____

_____

_____

CELEBRATING

Your Heritage

and your Spirit

"We are from the most incredible people in the history of humankind. I mean, social Darwinism, survival of the fittest, we are it. Ain't nobody been through what we've been through and we're still here to talk about it."

Hilary Beard
Author and NiaOnline Columnist

Celebrations of all kinds, from holidays to patriotic remembrances, cultural festivals, and religious rites, help shape who we are in the fabric of our families and society as a whole. What we celebrate and how we celebrate it are clear indications of our values and beliefs. One of the key steps a sister can take to keep her pride in the workplace is to celebrate our heritage during Black

History Month and to celebrate the African American holiday of Kwanzaa.

Celebrating Black History at Work

Ever since Carter G. Woodson got the country to recognize Negro History Week back in 1926, black folks have been making a concerted effort to acknowledge the gains that we as a people have made in this country. In 1976, the week was extended to a month, albeit the shortest month of the year. Currently, every February our nation honors the myriad accomplishments that are attributed to African Americans. Plenty of large corporations fund significant efforts during this period to bring light to deserving members of the black community.

However, as many "sole sisters" who are the only black person in their office will attest, Black History Month is not celebrated, or even understood, in every workplace. That reality leaves some African Americans feeling particularly uncomfortable when either trying to organize a Black History Month event at work or inviting colleagues to attend a celebration. They know that even in 2004, there are still people who say "so what?" to the notion of learning about our history and culture.

In response to that dismissive attitude, Janet Humdy Morrison, a senior trainer at Massachusetts-based Novations/J. Howard and Associates, suggests that a new way of thinking is long overdue in the corporate environment.

"It is unfortunate that the contributions of black Americans, women, and various ethnic groups have been underrepresented in our history books," she says. "We can use February as an opportunity to encourage the entire workforce to bring in and share information about contributions made by African Americans, particularly African Americans in business."

In a work environment where the concept of acknowledging Black History Month is welcomed, Morrison's suggestion may work brilliantly. In less-welcoming offices, however, you can imagine that some colleagues or supervisors would actually guffaw at the idea of having to do homework about African Americans to appease our interest in celebrating our achievements. Some people simply aren't going to care and may even become irritated by the suggestion that they engage in such an activity. Then what?

Convincing people to celebrate us for a month is actually beside the point, suggests Susan Cole Hill, who is vice president of human resources and communications at Disney Consumer Products. As the one who heads up the diversity program for the company in North America, she says, "I don't support tacos on Tuesday or black History celebrations in February or anything that panders to people. My interest is in real experiences that change the community or the workplace that you live in to make it easier for you to be productive and successful—to provide equal career opportunity."

To that end, Hill suggests a long-term strategy. "Always position yourself so that you have the opportunity to get the call for advancement," she counsels. "My assessment is certainly not to suggest that in an environment where you are the minority without being [appreciated], you should step out and say, 'I'm black, and I want to go out and be black on the one month that y'all allow me to be black.' That's crazy. It does not allow you to build any kind of support or other kind of engagement with the people who are a part of your real world. You can do that outside of the office."

Hill brings up a vital point for sisters in corporate America: your work cannot be your entire life. By establishing balance and cultivating relationships with friends and family, you can fulfill your cultural needs and desires separately, if necessary, while remaining on track at work. This doesn't mean diminishing who you are; more, it means strategizing about how you live your life.

For those of you who are unwilling to let go of your desire to convert your ornery coworkers, ask yourselves, "To what extent do I want to alienate everybody else because I want to celebrate my black identity?" You really can enjoy your cultural heritage someplace else. For those who do work in environments that embrace you, she recommends picking an event rich in heritage and history that can be nurturing and fulfilling for everybody's experience, not just your own black experience.

The bottom line is to remember where you are, who you are, and who is in your company. The reality is that you'll still be black in March! Create a meaningful celebration of our culture for yourself this month that will result in the continuing respect of those around you come March 1.

Look to Kwanzaa

Are you one of the millions of people who make a New Year's resolution every year, only to forget it by the end of January or just stop trying because other concerns get in the way?

Part of the reason for the high failure rate of committing to live whatever resolution you affirm is that resolutions generally emerge in haste. If you have ever found yourself contemplating what single thing you can do to turn around your work life, you can always look to your heritage for support.

Look specifically to Kwanzaa, the uniquely African American cultural celebration that starts the day after Christmas and ends on New Year's Day. Kwanzaa focuses celebrants' awareness on principles of honorable living that embrace the power, structure, and strength of the African American community.

You can use several of these principles to guide your steps at work into the new year. If you honestly engage them, they will work. Following are four of the seven principles to jump-start your resolution making. To learn about the three other Kwanzaa principles, read *Coming Together: Celebrations for African American Families*, by Harriette Cole and John Pinderhughes (Jump Sun, 2003).

UMOJA (UNITY)

One woman described to me how bitter she had become at work because the other black employees didn't speak to her. At first she went out of her way to talk to them—especially the executives—but then she just stopped. This made her feel even more alone and isolated in a predominantly white environment.

If this has happened to you, review your own actions. Do you act as a team player? Do you seek out ways to support yourself and those with whom you work? Do you make an effort to get to know the other African American employees, regardless of their job status? Or are you more interested in rising up the corporate ladder and making connections solely with those you believe are in power?

In the spirit of *umoja*, acknowledge other people of color at work—but do so genuinely, out of a true belief that you are all part of a larger culture. Similarly, adopt the approach of unity as it relates to every one of your coworkers. Assume the positive. Be kind first. Be thoughtful first.

Make the resolution to make eye contact with people of all backgrounds with whom you feel an affinity. Offer a smile of acknowledgment and keep on walking. This doesn't mean that you should behave naively. Remember all the while to stay strong on the inside so that people's responses don't shake you one way or the other.

KUJICHAGULIA (SELF-DETERMINATION)

Have you ever felt stuck in your job, with nowhere to turn? At that point, many people start pointing fingers. Somebody else is obviously to blame for what's going wrong with your career, right? Not necessarily.

Rather than succumb to a "woe is me" state of mind, contemplate the meaning of self-determination. What can you do for your own work life to improve your status? Should you go to night school to brush up on your computer skills?

What about deciding to read a book a month that will help hone your understanding about topics pertinent to your line of work? If you're feeling isolated, commit to going to networking events and putting yourself out there to meet like-minded people who are interested in growing in your career area.

NIA (PURPOSE)

Too often sisters complain about not getting their work done in the course of the day—either because of the many assignments that their boss has piled on them, or the personal challenges that occupy too much space in their minds.

Ultimately, lack of productivity points to a lack of purpose. For example, many highly successful sisters know that it's best to make a plan for your day the night before so that when you get up in the morning, you can execute your plan rather than figure it out as the day unfolds.

This one commitment can save you time and money because it centers you. Planning your day—everything from meditating in the morning and eating breakfast, to finishing a specific list of tasks at work and leaving in time to have a quality experience in the evening—aligns you with your purpose. It even works when you get surprise projects piled on your plate that you must add in at the last minute.

KUUMBA (CREATIVITY)

If you find yourself falling into a rut as the year closes, or on any day of your work life, refresh yourself. Remember your innate creativity and capabilities. This single power can serve as your fuel year-round.

Devise simple or dramatic ways to incorporate your creativity into your working life, too, so that you support yourself and others without exerting an overabundance of effort. Make or purchase a necklace, for example, inscribed with an inspiring word or phrase, or customize your computer's screen saver (that you will see daily) to remind yourself of your personal goals.

Decide to do something joyous for yourself each month that will reinvigorate your interest in your career. You might host a discussion group with people of different backgrounds to talk about art, philosophy, culture, music—

not necessarily topics related to your job, but ones that trigger creative thinking among peers. Often this leads to creative thinking at work.

Consider focusing on each principle of Kwanzaa during those last six days of this year and the first day of the next. Come January 2, you may be surprised by how easily your commitment to doing something great for your career will be manifested.

Resources

Novations/J. Howard & Associates
Brighton Landing West
10 Guest St.
Suite 300
Brighton, MA 02135
Phone: (617) 254-7600
Fax: (617) 254-7117
Email: info@jhoward.com
http://www.novations.com/

BOOKS ON KWANZAA

**Coming Together: Celebrations for
African American Families**
by Harriette Cole and John Pinderhughes
(Jump Sun, 2003)

**A Plentiful Harvest: Creating Balance and
Harmony Through the Seven Living Virtues**
by Terrie Williams
(Warner Books, 2002)

**Kwanzaa: An African American
Celebration of Culture and Cooking**
by Eric V. Copage
(Quill, 1993)

BLACK HISTORY INFORMATION RESOURCES

**1001 Things Everyone Should Know
About African American History**
by Jeffrey C. Stewart
(Main Street Books, 1997)

The African American Century: How Black Americans Have Shaped Our Country
by Henry Louis Gates Jr. and Cornel West
(Free Press, 2000)

African American Lives
by Henry Louis Gates Jr. and
Evelyn Brooks Higginbotham
(Oxford University Press, 2004)

Africana: The Encyclopedia of the African and African American Experience: The Concise Desk Reference
by Henry Louise Gates Jr. and Anthony Kwame Appiah
(Running Press Book Publishers, 2003)

The Atlas of African American History and Politics: From the Slave Trade to Modern Times
by Arwin D. Smallwood and Jeffrey M. Elliot
(McGraw-Hill, 1997)

The Autobiography of an Ex-Colored Man
by James Weldon Johnson
(Dover, 1995)

Before the Mayflower: A History of Black America
by Lerone Bennett Jr.
(Penguin, 1993)

Black Americans
by Alphonso Pinkney
(Pearson Education, 1999)

Black History Month Resource Book
by Mary Ellen Snodgrass
(Gale Group, 1998)

Black Movements in America (Revolutionary Thought/Radical Movements)
by Cedric J. Robinson
(Routledge, 1997)

From Babylon to Timbuktu: A History of the Ancient Black Races Including the Black Hebrews
by Rudolph R. Windsor
(Exposition Press, 1969)

The Bondwoman's Narrative
by Hannah Crafts and Henry Louis Gates Jr.
(Warner Books, 2003)

Darkwater: Voices From Within the Veil
by W. E. B. Du Bois and Manning Marable
(Dover, 1999)

**From Slavery to Freedom:
A History of African Americans**
by John Hope Franklin and Alfred A. Moss
(Knopf, 2000)

I Have a Dream: 24 Writings and Speeches That Changed the World
by Martin Luther King Jr. and James W. Washington
(HarperCollins, 1992)

Incidents in the Life of a Slave Girl
by Harriet A. Jacobs
(Dover, 2001)

Introduction to African Civilizations
by John G. Jackson and Runoko Rashidi
(Citadel Press, 2001)

**Narrative of the Life of Frederick Douglass,
An American Slave: Written by Himself**
by Frederick Douglass, John W. Blassingame,
John R. McKivigan, Peter P. Hinks, and Gerald Fulkerson
(Yale Nota Bene, 2001)

The Narrative of Sojourner Truth
by Olive Gilbert and Sojourner Truth
(Dover, 1997)

**The New York Public Library
African American Desk Reference**
by the New York Public Library
(Wiley, 1999)

**Sister Days: 365 Inspired Moments in
African American Women's History**
by Janus Adams
(Wiley, 2000)

**Unchained Memories:
Readings from the Slave Narratives**
by Cynthia Goodman and Spencer Crew
(Bulfinch, 2003)

Up From Slavery
by Booker T. Washington
(Dover, 1995)

TAKE NOTE:

How Will the Kwanzaa Principles Shape Your Career?

Let Kwanzaa be your career guide. Using the notes section below, jot down how you plan to incorporate the following seven principles, Nguzo Saba, into your work life:

1. Umoja (Unity)

_____

_____

_____

2. Kujichagulia (Self-Determination)

_____

_____

_____

3. Ujima (Collective Work and Responsibility)

_____

_____

_____

4. Ujamaa (Cooperative Economics)

_____

_____

_____

5. Nia (Purpose)

_____

_____

_____

6. Kuumba (Creativity)

_____

_____

_____

7. Imani (Faith)

_____

_____

_____

PART 2

A SISTER'S MAP TO
THE CORPORATE MINEFIELD

GET PAID

What You're *Really* Worth

Many of us are living single and raising families on our own. On top of that, we are pulling double duty at work: it's a documented fact that women—especially sisters—often earn less than men for doing the same work but put in longer hours. You're probably sick and tired of working a nine-to-five (or longer, in many cases) job only to make ends meet. You know you are worth more than the dollar amount on your paycheck. The big question is, how can a sister get paid?

The burden of increasing your salary falls on your shoulders. Too many women, however, are afraid to ask for a raise. Your employer isn't going to increase your salary just because you want to buy a new car or need to pay off student loans. But you could be in a very good position for a raise if you can demonstrate that an idea you implemented cut costs or increased sales, for instance, or you've taken on additional responsibilities since you were hired.

Be Prepared

As the Girl Scout motto states, be prepared. When you request a raise, you can expect your supervisor to respond in one of five ways. Below, we've listed those typical responses, along with counterresponses to help you get paid.

Do you think you're being paid what you're worth at work?

Yes   58 (20%)

No   184 (61%)

I'm not sure   22 (7%)

I'm not currently working   36 (12%)

Results of a July 2004 online poll of 300 members of NiaOnline's Consumer Advisory Panel. All respondents were black women eighteen and over.

RESPONSE #1

Boss: You don't deserve a raise because you haven't worked here long enough.

You: My contribution to the company can't be adequately measured by the amount of time I've been here.

Advice: State why you deserve a raise, backed by documentation.

RESPONSE #2

Boss: You deserve a raise, but the company can't afford it.

You: Can you agree to my request for a raise with the understanding that it won't take effect until a specified date in the future?

Advice: You could propose a 5 percent hike immediately, followed by another 5 percent raise in six months. Here's one alternative response:

You: Instead of an actual salary increase, can you raise the overall value of my compensation [meaning things including more vacation time; a flexible work schedule, such as working from home; tuition reimbursement; or whatever else meets your needs]?

RESPONSE #3

Boss: You deserve a raise, but my hands are tied because of company policy.

You: Does this mean that no matter how hard I work or how much responsibility I take on, I won't be rewarded for it?

Advice: Instead of waiting for a response, say you had hoped that performance would be rewarded in the company. Then restate justifiable reasons for a pay raise.

RESPONSE #4

Boss: You deserve everything you have asked for; you get the raise.

Advice: Once you've made your thank-yous, get everything in writing. Also, if your boss didn't put up a fight, it may be because you asked for too little. Unless you know your true worth—your market value—you could get stuck with a token salary increase. For salary calculators and surveys, check out WetFeet.com and JobStar.org.

RESPONSE #5

Boss: No.

Advice: If your boss turns you down flat, consider looking for a new job. You can always ask her or him what you would need to do to earn a raise. But remember that you are negotiating for a raise based on your hard work, not begging for more money.

To make a persuasive argument for why you deserve a raise, you must show not only that you are putting in the extra effort (such as staying late and taking on extra work) but also that those efforts havc had a positive impact on productivity and profitability. If you have done all of this and still are not getting the salary you want and deserve, you need to read the following tips from career consultant and coach Debra Brown, who runs the New York-based Workforce America, part of the Five O'Clock Club:

1. **Seek out the mole.** Make a connection with folks at your company who may be able to give you an idea of how other folks are being paid. Doing this is not as difficult as it sounds. You may discover you came in at a lower salary than other people at your level. You don't want to ask anyone directly what she or he makes, but you can ask about salary ranges at the company.

2. **Name it and claim it.** If you are not earning as much as men (or white folks) in similar jobs at the firm, arrange a meeting with your boss and say, "After doing some fact-gathering on my own with respect to people with functions similar to mine, it seems to me that I am really off the bell curve in terms of compensation. Any idea what may account for that?"

3. **Expose the dirty linen.** If your boss becomes flustered and appears to be at a loss for words, follow up with, "I have been looking at glass-ceiling reports from organizations such as Catalyst [if it's a women's issue] and the NAACP [if it's related to race], and wage disparity between men and women [or white people and minorities] is pervasive. As an African American female, I'm interested in finding out whether anyone has ever done a glass-ceiling review of this company." Your boss was

probably assuming that you would be much too polite—and much too political—to mention this.

4. **Keep a paper trail.** Follow up by sending a dated email (with a return receipt requested) saying, "Thank you so much for our meeting. I really appreciate being in an environment where I feel safe enough to talk about my concerns regarding perhaps inadvertent disparities in salary treatment." This way it doesn't sound as if you are about to litigate. Document anything that looks retaliatory and may be actionable.

5. **Peel back the onion.** Give your boss a chance to respond. Look for any "issues." For instance, was he or she patronizing you by telling you that you're doing a great job, while thinking that you're doing a great job "for a black person"? By that standard, management may feel that you are being paid commensurate with its lowered performance expectations for black folks.

6. **Speak your mind.** What if a white person whom you have trained moves ahead of you? Say to your boss, "When Mary Jane came in, I was asked to provide her with information that she needed to know to perform her duties. I was told I did a great job. But it seems that the reward for my coaching is that she was able to present my information to a more responsive audience, and I was ignored. Now I see that Mary Jane has been promoted. Can you help me understand this situation better?"

7. **Stay cool, calm, and collected.** Your boss may expect you to suppress your rage out of fear that by protesting, you'll be jeopardizing your job. And indeed, you may be thinking, "Gee, there is going to be that time when I need to

leave early because my kid is sick, or I get stuck in traffic and I'm an hour late to work." On the other hand, your boss may expect you to blow up so that he or she can go after you for being belligerent or insubordinate.

What your boss does not expect you to do is to calmly and methodically seek out information that helps determine whether your suspicions are correct.

8. **Take it as far as necessary.** What if you've had your discussions with your employer, created a paper trail, and met all of the criteria that management has set forth—and still nothing happens? It's time to go to human resources, the company's diversity committee, or whomever else you think has leverage within the firm. Only after you've explored these avenues should you take the next step, which is to present your case to the U.S. Equal Employment Opportunity Commission (EEOC). What you should not do is go quietly into that good night. Make it a painful, and memorable, experience for your employer so that the folks coming after you won't have to fight the same battle over and over again.

Resources

Catalyst
120 Wall St., 5th Floor
New York, NY 10005
Phone: (212) 514-7600
Fax: (212) 514-8470
Email: info@catalystwomen.org
http://www.catalystwomen.org/

NAACP
4805 Mt. Hope Dr.
Baltimore MD 21215
Phone: (877) NAACP-98
24-Hour Hotline: (410) 521-4939
http://www.naacp.org/

WetFeet, Inc.
609 Mission St., Suite 400
San Francisco, CA 94105
Phone: (415) 284-7900
Fax: (415) 284-7910
http://wetfeet.com/

JobStar
http://jobstar.org/
Visit the Jobstar website for contact
information and for locations of local,
national, and worldwide career resources.

Workforce America
Candidate Resources, Inc.
2100 Hwy 360, Suite 400-B
Grand Prairie, TX 75050
Phone: (972) 641-5494 x199
Fax: (972) 641-5647
Email: mcotter@criw.com
http://www.workforceamerica.org/

The Five O'Clock Club
300 East 40th St., Suite 6L
New York, NY 10016
Phone: (212) 286-9332 x600
http://www.fiveoclockclub.com/

Compensation
Self Quiz

Are you getting paid what you deserve? Take the Compensation Self-Quiz to find out if you're getting fairly compensated for the work you do. Then, read the profile based on your score. When answering question one, if you don't know the market rate salary range for your position, visit Careerbuildier.com or SalaryExpert.com to get an estimate.

1. **How does your current salary match up to the market salary range?**
   a. Equal to the market rate salary range for your position and length of tenure. **1** point
   b. 5 percent below the market rate salary range for your position and length of tenure. **2** points
   c. 10 percent below the market rate salary range for your position and length of tenure. **3** points
   d. 15 percent below the market rate salary range for your position and length of tenure. **4** points
   Score _____

2. **Have you observed a pattern of unequal pay or unfair promotion based on gender or race in your workplace?**
   a. I really can't say. **0** point
   b. No. **0** point
   c. Yes. **2** points
   Score _____

3. **Have your previous requests for pay increases
   been rejected?**
   a. No, my requests have been met. **0 points**
   b. I've never asked before. **0 points**
   c. Yes, my request was denied once before. **1 point**
   d. Yes, my requests have been denied
      several times. **3 points**
   Score _____

4. **When you started working at your current job, was your pay
   equal to the pay of others starting at the same position and
   with similar experience?**
   a. I don't have enough information to judge. **0 points**
   b. Yes, my pay was about equal to the pay of my peers.
      0 points
   c. No, my pay was higher than the pay of my peers.
      0 points
   d. No, my pay was lower than the pay of my peers.
      4 points
   Score _____

5. **Have a number of colleagues or coworkers doing similar
   work but of lower seniority been promoted or given raises
   ahead of you?**
   a. I don't have enough information to judge. **0 points**
   b. No, I've consistently been given raises and/or promo-
      tions ahead of coworkers of lower seniority. **0 points**
   c. One or two coworkers of lower seniority have been
      given raises and/or promotions ahead of me. **2 points**
   d. A number of coworkers of lower seniority have been
      given raises and/or promotions ahead of me. **4 points**
   Score _____

Total all four scores _____

If you scored 1–6 points: Unless you've been doing a lot of extra work or feel that you deserve a pay increase for reasons not captured in this quiz, it seems that things are pretty straightforward: you're getting paid what you feel comfortable with and you're likely getting paid what you deserve.

If you scored 7–17 points: You're in a zone of suspicion, which means you'll need to get more information to justify any suspicions you might have regarding whether you are being fairly compensated.

If you answered b. or c. to question one, talk to your boss or manager and find out why you are being paid below the market rate salary range for your position and length of tenure. You'll have to follow your instincts here. If your manager gives you an explanation that corresponds with reality—your relative lack of experience or knowledge compared to your better-paid colleagues, for example—ask him or her what you can do to "catch up" and agree to a benchmark date when you can revisit the salary issue. If you answered d. to question one, you should consider having a serious conversation with your boss about your salary. Unless your company can justify such a gross division between the salary of your peers and your salary—say, if there is provable evidence of lack of skills or even incompetence on your part—you should consider quitting or even taking legal action.

If you answered c. to question two, it's time to pull out the big guns. An observable pattern of unequal pay or unfair promotion based on gender or race in your workplace is sufficient basis for you to contact Catalyst or the NAACP and/or to contact a lawyer. If you're not the only sister in the office, or if the pattern you observe affects other minorities or women, try to feel out whether your colleagues are observing the same thing. If you all agree that something's going on, you'll bring a stronger case to your company's management by working as a team or group than pushing forward on compensatory action on your own.

If you answered c. or d. to question three, you can play it two ways. If your request was denied once before, you may feel that the rejection was justified and based on a fair assessment of the situation. You might choose not to take action. If you don't feel that that rejection was fair, you should follow the advice given in the previous chapter. If your request was denied several times, you should really evaluate either your employer's commitment to you and/or your commitment to your employer.

If you answered d. to question four, you should consider bringing up the topic of starting pay either during a meeting you set up or during your regular salary review. If your manager can't come up with a good, reasonable explanation for why your starting salary is lower than that of your peers, you should ask him or her why that is the case.

If you answered c. or d. to question five, you have two options. If one or two coworkers of lower seniority have been given raises and/or been promoted ahead of you, it's possible there is a reasonable explanation. Find out what it is. Ask your boss what it is about the performance of your colleagues that got them raises and promotion ahead of you. Again, go with your gut. If there's a reasonable basis to the explanation—say, work above and beyond expectations that your colleagues performed and that you did not—than you can try to catch up by doing extra work or you can decide that your organization is not worth that extra effort. If, on the other hand, you discover that a number of coworkers of lower seniority have been given raises and/or promoted ahead of you, you should talk to your boss about this and find out if the organization is committed to your continuing employment.

5

WHAT TO DO
WHEN YOU SUSPECT
Bias in the
Workplace

"Having grown up in the civil rights era, having entered the workforce in 1969, there was never any doubt in my mind that racism and sexism were going to be factors in my life. I am somewhat surprised when I encounter younger women who are not prepared for racism and sexism . . . I really think that because racism and sexism are so prevalent, we have to be able to use the fact that we are women and women of color of our advantage. [Others] want to see it as a negative and therefore they set the bar low. They don't know what we can accomplish."

Paula Sneed
Group Vice President of Kraft Foods

There are few greater hazards in the corporate minefield than facing sexual or racial discrimination (or both). They can stop you dead in your tracks, and they're extremely tough to disarm without having them blow up in your face.

Federal law prohibits employment discrimination based on race, color, religion, sex, or national origin. It also protects men and women who perform "substantially equal work" in the same workplace from gender-based wage discrimination. However, in a 2001 survey by *The Washington Post*, the Henry J. Kaiser Family Foundation, and Harvard University, more than a third of all blacks interviewed said they had been rejected for a job or failed to win a promotion because of their race. Gender-based discrimination also persists.

If you believe you have been a victim of workplace discrimination, your options, in escalating order, include:

1. **Seeking a remedy within your company**

2. **Filing a complaint with the U.S. Equal Employment Opportunity Commission (EEOC)**

3. **Filing a civil lawsuit**

In fact, your success with options two and three usually depend upon the completion of the first option.

NiaOnline spoke to Chey Blake, a New York–based attorney with a background in employment law, to find out what you should do if you believe you are a victim of workplace discrimination.

Discrimination claims are very difficult to prove, cautions Blake. Indeed, in 2003 more than two-thirds of race-based complaints and 57 percent of sex-based complaints filed with the EEOC were determined to have "no reasonable cause." "Employers are more savvy now about how to handle such claims and discrimination is a lot more subtle. You're unlikely to find the smoking gun, such as a boss who says, 'women shouldn't be paid as much as men.' Nevertheless, you must be able to prove that the offenses are sex- or race-based, and not just that the boss doesn't like you," says Blake.

Furthermore, the aftermath of a successful claim can be unpleasant if you wish to remain in the environment where you were victimized. "By law your employer can't retaliate against you for filing an EEOC complaint. However, if you have a really contentious battle with your company, and the goal is to keep your job, think of what kind of environment you will be working in afterward," says Blake.

For this reason, "you must be very clear about what you want out of this before going forward," she cautions. Do you want a promotion for which you believe you were unfairly passed over? Do you want a job for which you think you were unjustly turned down? Are you seeking compensation because you believe you're being paid less than a white man who is doing the same job? "Focus on what specific remedies you want, not just on getting 'justice,'" says Blake.

Once you've decided what you want, Blake suggests the following steps:

> **Has racism stopped you from getting ahead in the workplace?**
>
> **Yes** it has kept me from getting ahead 90 (30%)
>
> **No** I haven't been a victim of racism in the workplace 71 (24%)
>
> **Bias is there,** but it hasn't stopped my progress 115 (38%)
>
> **I'm not sure** 24 (8%)

Results of a July 2004 online poll of 300 members of NiaOnline's Consumer Advisory Panel. All respondents were black women eighteen and over.

1. **Keep a meticulous paper trail.** "If you decide to file a complaint with the EEOC, it's a fact-based inquiry and so you have collect your facts: times, dates, who did what, who said what, what you think it means, anything that you can gather, organized in chronological order." Save emails and memos. When you believe a discriminatory event has occurred, note down the time, date, place, and who was present.

2. **Make sure your record is stellar.** "You need to be squeaky clean," insists Blake. That means you have not broken company policies or displayed poor work habits, such as habitually arriving late for work. "Anything that you're doing that employers can point to in order to justify their behavior, they will. The 'they let Sally do that, why can't I?' defense will not help you very much, because if you have broken company policy—even if they didn't enforce it against someone else—you still broke it." Make sure you keep copies of your employee reviews in order to show that you have been a good employee.

3. **Seek internal remedies first, but be quick about it.** Many companies have internal policies on how employee complaints should be handled. "Even if you think those procedures won't result in assistance, you want to bring your concerns to your employer's attention. Don't leave the argument open that the employer would have remedied the problem if he had known about it," says Blake. If there's no set policy within your company, it's advisable to seek a lawyer's advice, and then talk with your boss and/or the human resources department. Avoid the D-word, however, if you're thinking of taking your claim further, because it will give your employer a head start in

preparing a defense. Just talk about the actions that concern you, without describing what you believe are the discriminatory reasons behind them.

If you plan to go further, don't waste too much time on this step, cautions Blake. You must exhaust all your internal remedies before contacting the EEOC; however, the EEOC must be contacted within forty-five days of the most recent discriminatory action.

4. **Seek legal advice.** Get a lawyer's assistance to make sure that you can state your claim clearly and convincingly. "What people find to be emotionally hurtful or offensive is not necessarily a legal offense," explains Blake. "People who even have legitimate complaints tend to focus on the wrong things, the most hurtful things to them, when what may seem like a minor point is the real legal offense."

5. **Contact an EEOC counselor.** Before filing a complaint with the EEOC, you must undergo counseling on the commission's procedures and the remedies that are available to you, such as alternative dispute resolution or filing a complaint. To find your local EEOC office and speak to a counselor, call the New York office at (800) 669-4000 or visit the website at www.eeoc.gov. Counseling must be completed within thirty days of the date that you contacted the counselor.

6. **File an EEOC complaint.** If the matter is not resolved during the counseling period, the EEOC counselor must inform you, in writing, of the right to file a discrimination complaint. Your complaint must be filed within fifteen days of that notice. The EEOC must complete its

investigation within 180 days of a complaint; however, you have the right to amend your complaint to reflect later instances of discrimination, in which case the investigation must be complete within 360 days of your original complaint. Within that time the commission may dismiss the complaint. Barring dismissal, you have the right to request a hearing. If the commission's final decision is not to your liking, you have the right to appeal within thirty days.

"Generally within six to nine months you will be through the system," says Blake. "If your claim has merit they will go to your employer with remedies." Those remedies can include back pay, hiring, promotion, reinstatement, and other actions that will help to even out the playing field.

7. **File a civil lawsuit.** Once the EEOC process is complete, if you are not satisfied with the result, you may file a civil action in federal court against your employer, usually within ninety days. There are exceptions in which you may not have to go through the EEOC first. Consult with your attorney about these.

Addressing workplace discrimination can be an uphill battle, but take heart—companies are paying the price if they tolerate discrimination. Corporate giants such as Boeing and Morgan Stanley have recently agreed to pay out multimillion-dollar settlements to class-action lawsuits by female employees who alleged that employers or coworkers had discriminated against them at work.

6

TURN YOUR
Setbacks Into Comebacks

"Do not confuse aptitude with attitude when pursuing success; both are essential. The reality is that only 20 percent of success is related to your aptitude, and 80 percent of your success is your attitude."

Candace Matthews
President of SoftSheen-Carson

There's an old saying: "When life gives you lemons, make lemonade." It may be cliché, but it still resonates with truth. Among the many success stories out there are those of sisters who were poverty stricken but who are now living large, such as media mogul Oprah Winfrey. Or what about those who had it all, lost it, and got it all back again, such as singer Tina Turner during her post-Ike Turner success in the 1980s? People often forget that author Terry McMillan at one time was practically selling books door-to-door at local churches before her work hit the bestseller list.

Perhaps you have run into a stumbling block or have taken a wrong turn in your career, and you don't know how to get back on track. Whether you have missed out on a job promotion, amassed a lot of debt, or failed at a new business venture, the key to moving forward is staying motivated and empowering yourself to take control of a bad situation.

If you feel you have failed or been defeated, you may experience the same kinds of emotions you'd have if you lost a loved one. First there is shock, then denial, fear, anger, depression, and, finally, acceptance, according to psychologist Don Greene, PhD, author of *Fight Your Fear and Win: Seven Skills for Performing Your Best Under Pressure—At Work, in Sports, on Stage* (Broadway, 2002). Once you've accepted your situation, Greene adds, the next step is realizing that there is no quick fix-it formula. The best approach is to take your comeback one day at a time, with a positive attitude. You must find a way to turn every setback into a comeback.

The foundation of every comeback is built on a good strategic plan. Having a concrete plan and goals will help you to avoid feeling stuck. You should be very clear about what it is you want—whether it's a senior-management position, early retirement, or your own business.

You should also map out the steps that will help you carry out your plan, in addition to keeping a record of your own progress. At the same time, you need a contingency plan for handling situations that could derail you. The following examples offer some guidance:

Career woes: Let's say you want to be a part of senior management, but you were recently turned down for a promotion. Maybe you need to redefine yourself to your colleagues or increase your visibility internally among key decision makers. Or you could lack the skills needed to succeed in senior management—but that doesn't mean you can't develop those skills. A career coach or even a mentor can help you assess your career path and redefine your goals. Bear in mind that getting to that next step could take a few months or even several years, depending on the gaps that need to be filled between your current position and the one you desire. (In Part Three of this guide, Tips for Taking It to the Next Level, you can learn more about career coaches and mentors.)

Financial blues: Too many sisters are deeply in debt. But how do you get out from under that particular mountain? One way to accelerate the rate at which your debt is paid off is to start paying more than the minimum due. This way, more of your payment goes toward the principal balance rather than just the interest.

Too often, people think debt consolidation is a quick fix, but it isn't. All you're doing in this case is transferring your debt from one company to another. And often it takes longer to pay off the loan. Look at the terms of the loan before you sign for it; the interest rate and monthly payment should be lower than what you are currently paying. If you do get such a loan, make sure you close out the accounts you paid off with the loan so you don't rack up new charges. If you are unable to pay all of your bills on time, contact the Federal Trade Commission's Consumer

Response Center at www.ftc.gov or (877) 382-4357 for more advice on paying off debt.

Business challenges: One mistake many folks make in running a business is trying to go it alone. Even before you run into problems, you should seek help. A great resource is SCORE (Service Corps of Retired Executives). With more than 11,000 volunteer business counselors, SCORE provides small-business mentoring and advice for free. A SCORE counselor is a business expert who has firsthand experience owning or operating your type of business. You can meet face-to-face or get email counseling 24-7. SCORE business counselors are also well versed in developing effective business plans. Go to www.score.org or call (800) 634-0245.

Another resource: community-based business incubators. In addition to providing low-cost space, these might offer management training, technical assistance, and financing. For a list of incubators, contact the National Business Incubation Association at www.nbia.org or (740) 593-4331.

One thing you know for sure is that change is constant. You have to be willing to accept and adjust to the unpredictable, whether it lies within the personal or the professional area of your life. The key is finding a way to make these life occurrences work for you instead of against you.

TAKE NOTE:

What's Your Comeback Plan?

Using the notes section below, take a few moments to start shaping the strategic plan that will take you to better days. Start by listing all of the areas you want to improve, in order of importance to you. It's vital to prioritize your concerns, because attempting to take on all of life's problems at one time will leave you feeling overwhelmed and defeated.

Start at the top of the list and write down one action you will take to address that concern. Then take that action.

Keep revisiting the list, addressing each concern one by one, and then crossing off actions when they're completed. Soon you'll be on your way to your big comeback.

_____

_____

_____

_____

_____

_____

_____

_____

_____

_____

_____

_____

_____

_____

_____

_____

_____

_____

_____

_____

_____

_____

_____

_____

_____

_____

_____

FIGURE OUT

Whether It's Time *to* Move On

Sometimes you reach the top of your career ladder only to find that you're no longer on the correct ladder. Writer Hilary Beard, who informs NiaOnline readers about health matters, was in that position several years ago. During the 2004 Nia Enterprises Leadership Summit in New York, she described how after graduating with honors from an Ivy League university, then advancing through sales, market-ing, and general management positions with large compa-nies, she felt stifled by her corporate success.

"At that point in time I was with PepsiCo doing new business development for them. And for years I had just been dreaming of transitioning into a life where I would have more autonomy and could be more creative," Beard said. "But I was afraid to leave my job. I was afraid that I would lose my financial security...I was afraid that I would spoil a wonderful-looking resume. I was afraid that if I left and didn't succeed, I wouldn't be able to go back.

"Little did I know that I would never *want* to go back," she added.

Beard quietly dropped out of a graduate business program that she had been attending and began to take creative writing classes in the evenings. She and two other similarly situated coworkers also began an informal support group to encourage each other to pursue their dreams. "We would meet on a monthly basis and we even wrote strategic plans for ourselves," Beard said. Then she would take small steps to follow her plan. "Once I started identifying things that weren't too scary to do, I started to build my confidence and began to take bigger and bigger steps. And then opportunities came at me so quickly that a five-year plan turned into a one-year plan...I had no idea that my skills from corporate America would translate into a creative life and help me transition so quickly."

Beard left PepsiCo in 1997 to launch chapter two of her career, as a journalist. "I transitioned into a life that was more wonderful than I ever could have imagined. Shockingly, to me, by the second year of working for myself, I was earning a salary that was equivalent to my corporate salary," remarked Beard. "Now I feel I can really take care of myself. I believe that this transition has really strengthened me and will extend my life because I've found balance mentally, physically, and spiritually."

Are you ready for your own chapter two? Ask yourself these questions: Am I existing rather than living? Am I working just to earn money rather than for real job satisfaction? If you answered yes to either one, chances are you're in a rut and it's time to get yourself out of it. We may not decide to change jobs until a work situation becomes unbearable. By the time we reach this point, we feel desperate and are willing to take the next thing that comes along, which might not be any better than the situation we left. But you don't have to reach that breaking point. Here's how to evaluate your own situation, take charge, and make all the right moves:

> **Do you consider your work to be a J-O-B, or a J-O-Y?**
>
> **J-O-B** 149 (50%)
> **J-O-Y** 92 (30%)
> **Doesn't matter, it pays the bills** 59 (20%)

Results of a July 2004 online poll of 300 members of NiaOnline's Consumer Advisory Panel. All respondents were black women eighteen and over.

Decide whether you're staying or going—or evolving. People often start chapter two by leaving their employer, but shifting gears doesn't necessarily mean having to resign. You may choose to stay put but manage your career differently. This could include applying for a new position within your company or working out a deal to trade the tasks that don't match your strengths for a great project that does.

You could also opt to do freelance work on the side. On the other hand, you may decide that you need to change careers altogether. Perhaps you even want to start your own business. It's up to you. The only thing you shouldn't do is nothing.

Think about what job you really want. Deep down, we all know what we want to do. What keeps us from admitting it is the belief that it's unattainable. We tell ourselves we couldn't possibly run our own company or write books.

Don't be your own biggest obstacle to career fulfillment. If you have trouble deciding what to do, read *What Color Is Your Parachute? A Practical Guide for Job-Hunters and Career*

Changers by Richard Nelson Bolles (Ten Speed Press; $17.95). Also check out resources at CareerPlanner.com.

Look for a job in a hot field, but only if it's a good fit for you. Uncover thorough information about prospective fields by networking, reading, and doing online research. Informally interview fellow college alumni, friends, family, and associates to get the scoop. Don't overlook professional trade magazines.

Start a sideline business. Beginning your own paid or unpaid side project might help you take your mind off what's bringing you down while leading you to discover your true talents and interests.

Launch a full-time enterprise. If you have three to six months' worth of basic living expenses in the bank and access either to loans or to help from family and friends for start-up costs, then you might just want to strike out on your own.

Set goals and a time limit for achieving them. Do something every day toward reaching your goals. Make a phone call, write a letter, send out your resume, do research—whatever is needed.

You'll need a strong support system, so be sure to let friends, family, and colleagues advise you about critical issues. And don't expect a transformation overnight. Writing a new chapter in your life takes time.

Five Signs That It's Time To Move On From Your Job

Sometimes we feel the need to make a change, and sometimes change comes to us uninvited. Either way, change is difficult for most of us, so we often ignore the signals telling us it's time to move on. Here are five signs that it may be time to start thinking about your other options, even at a job that you enjoy:

> **Who is held back more by racism: black women or black men?**
>
> **Black men**   132 (44%)
> **Black women**   54 (18%)
> **We're held back equally**   100 (33%)
> **Neither gender is held back**   14 (5%)
>
> *Results of a July 2004 online poll of 300 members of NiaOnline's Consumer Advisory Panel. All respondents were black women eighteen and over.*

1. **The management no longer asks for your opinion.** If you are no longer invited to participate in meetings with key personnel where important decisions are made, you may have overstayed your welcome.

2. **The plum assignments keep going to other people.** Every time an opportunity comes up for a challenging assignment, it goes to someone else. It could be that you never told your boss that you wanted more challenging work. If this is the case, then speak up. However, if you have already mastered your job and it looks as if there is no chance of advancement, you need to find a job where there is room to grow.

3. **You are constantly passed over for a promotion.** Your company had been grooming you for a better position and had assured you that you were next in line. But instead, management fills the job with an outside candidate. Why? Perhaps there's been a company merger or strategic alliance, and your current skills are not in line with the company's new direction or structure. In this case, you need to ask your boss what you can do (such as get new training) to move forward with the company.

4. **Key personnel are leaving the company.** Do they know something you don't? Time to become a supersleuth and find out what is going on behind closed doors.

5. **You dread going to work.** You begin every weekend singing, "Thank God it's Friday." By Sunday night you're rapping, "Don't push me 'cause I'm close to the edge." Take some time off to get your head together or start looking for another job.

Don't let money be the reason you hang on to a job. There's a heavy price to pay for staying at a job you hate. According to Monster.com, workplace dissatisfaction and stress are the top two health problems for working adults.

8

IS IT TIME TO
Dust Off Your Resume?

Chances are that when you were entering the job market, your folks encouraged you to get a steady, secure job at an established company, and then to hold onto it for years to come. After all, that was the ideal situation when they were growing up, and many companies provided lifetime job security.

Not so today. In this era of corporate mergers, frequent layoffs, and jobs going overseas, you never know when you may be hitting the pavement again, resume in hand. But you'd be wise not to wait for an unforeseen crisis—such as having human resources hand you a pink slip—to dust the cobwebs off of that resume. Remember the old axiom: "The best time to search for a job is when you already have one."

Granted, reviewing your career history to reconstruct or update your resume can be a daunting task if you haven't done it in a while—which is all the more reason to do it when you aren't under any pressure to find a new job.

Your resume is your personal marketing tool, after all. After reading your own resume, you should be able to shout out, "I'd hire me!" If you can't say that with confidence, then you definitely need some help. A resume that isn't riveting has a life span of about fifteen seconds before getting tossed into the "reject" pile. Your job is to write one that gets you an interview. The following pointers will help you sell yourself even in a tight job market.

Abandon the one-page rule. The one-page resume was the standard format back in the 1980s, but that is no longer the case. The market is tight, and the number of downsized workers has made competition fierce. If you have an extensive work history, more than one college degree, or lots of special training or skills—or are very active in the community—then you shouldn't feel required to shrink everything down to six-point type in order to get it to fit on one page. The one-page resume can certainly do the job for recent grads, but for anyone who has been in the workplace for ten or more years, a two-page resume is now par for the course. One tip: put your contact info on both pages, in case they get separated.

Stay current with technology. We live in a fast-paced, tech-driven world. You should certainly have an email address that you can include as part of your contact information. Also, a potential employer may want to forgo snail mail and have you email your resume, so keep an electronic version of your resume, in plain text format.

Don't write an autobiography. You may feel compelled to show each move you've made along the way, often starting from your first job. While this approach may make sense for a chronological resume, it doesn't provide for a compelling one. Typically, employers do want to see a clear, linear path of professional experience related to the same work theme, so feel free to minimize unrelated work experience so that the relevant experience is highlighted. Also bear in mind that an ideal resume showcases skills rather than just recapping your job experience.

How do you feel about your job?
I love it!   69 (23%)
I like it somewhat   107 (36%)
I neither like nor dislike it   36 (12%)
I dislike it somewhat   37 (12%)
I hate it!   15 (5%)
I don't have one   36 (12%)

Results of a July 2004 online poll of 300 members of NiaOnline's Consumer Advisory Panel. All respondents were black women eighteen and over.

Make it user-friendly. Keep your resume concise and focus on your key selling points. Every word should be selling your credentials and showing your value to a potential employer. Emphasize recent achievements, higher-level functions, and experiences that are germane to your goal. Use a combination of paragraphs and bullets. For each job, provide a brief paragraph that details the scope of your responsibilities. Then create a bulleted list of your top contributions.

Tailor your document. You should create more than one version of your resume, depending on the types of jobs you are seeking. Your objective, or mission statement, at the top of resume should vary, of course, with the different versions. For each version of your resume, you may also choose to include or emphasize specific skills, certifications, professional affiliations, and experiences.

Quantify your achievements. Don't just recap job duties with no indication of actual job performance. Show that you constantly produced results. If you increased revenues from $250,000 in 1997 to $1.5 million in 2000, and tripled your client base, then say so! If you can't use actual dollar figures, cite percentages. What types of challenges did you face? Focus on money, time, and amounts. Emphasize how you have met deadlines. One concise, straightforward example: "I trained fifteen new employees on operations procedures."

Focus on your potential employer's needs, not your own. It is up to you to prepare a resume that meets a prospective employer's immediate needs. In presenting your credentials—career objectives, industry experience, scope of accomplishments, and education or training background—you must convince your audience that your combination of skills, experience, and initiative is exactly what they need. Note that this doesn't mean you should use inflated language. Let your accomplishments speak for themselves.

TAKE NOTE:

What Did You Accomplish At Work During The Past Year?

Using the notes section below, take a few moments to list three things you did on the job during the past year that went above and beyond the call of duty. These notes will be helpful during your next job interview, or even an annual review at your current place of employment.

_____

_____

_____

_____

_____

_____

_____

_____

_____

_____

_____

_____

_____

_____

_____

_____

_____

_____

_____

_____

_____

_____

_____

_____

_____

_____

_____

_____

_____

_____

_____

PART 3

TIPS FOR TAKING IT
TO THE NEXT LEVEL

9

ARE YOU

Selling Yourself Short?

"But really, dream big . . . what is the greatest you that you can become? Who is she? What does she do? What does she look like? How does she move in the world? What are her values? What does she stand for? That's how you become your own brand."

Harriette Cole
Life Coach and Nationally Syndicated Columnist

Branding isn't just for the self-employed. Even corporate professionals need to market themselves. You may have heard the term "branding" before, and understand how it relates to companies and entertainers. But how does it relate to someone who is holding down a nine-to-five job? Are there any specific branding strategies for people working in corporate America?

Absolutely. Branding may be associated more with Fortune 500 corporations and the Michael Jordans of the world, but anyone who wants to rise to the top of her field will have to do some self-promotion.

Praying that you will rise to the next level based on your performance alone isn't how it works these days. To achieve optimal career success, you will have to make yourself stand out from the crowd. Here are some sure-fire ways to achieve this goal:

Create high-profile opportunities. Seize any opportunity that will gain you recognition among your superiors and set you apart from the pack. Pay attention in staff meetings to requests or needs that aren't being met. Maybe there's a special project at work that, while not part of your job description, is something you are more than capable of doing. Will the work enhance your resume? If so, then take the initiative and do it. More than likely you'll be taking on more work and longer hours, but in the long run it will be worth it if you become branded as an expert and a leader.

Exhibit skills that establish you as an authority. Ask yourself this question: "Are the skills I bring to my job unique within my company, or are they pretty much like the skills of everyone else who has my job in this field?" If your qualifications don't stand out from the crowd, then you might want to consider attending a class either to brush up on your skills or to learn new ones. (Your next project will be to make sure everyone comes to associate your name with that new skill set.) Read trade papers or trade journals to keep up with what's going on in your industry so that you can always link your abilities to the market's need.

Align yourself with professional organizations. Professional and civic groups offer opportunities for you to showcase your talents. Get your name—and face—circulating in as many places as possible. Serve as chair of a committee in a professional organization to which you belong. Volunteer to coordinate an event. These types of activities allow you to be viewed as a manager and a valuable source of expertise.

Polish your presentation and public-speaking skills. There are groups such as Toastmasters that can help you get past any barriers to speaking in front of a group and gain the exposure you need as a speaker. Increase your visibility by volunteering to speak at industry seminars or participating in a panel discussion at public forums. You'll not only help prove your expertise to your employer; you'll also gain access to corporate sponsors and contacts that might be critical to your next career move. Teach a seminar or lecture at a local college. Also explore enrolling in an accredited program and becoming certified in your area of expertise.

Get published. Write an article for a professional journal or trade publication that will establish your credibility and solidify your authority among your peers. Get published or quoted in the company newsletter, newspapers, magazines, or scholarly journals. Pursue exposure on a local television or radio program, or even the company marketing video. Consider writing a book about what you know as another vehicle for establishing your expertise.

Resources

Toastmasters International
P.O. Box 9052
Mission Viejo, CA 92690
Phone: (949) 858-8255
http://www.toastmasters.org/

10

COULD YOUR

Career Use a Coach?

"I think we have to be comfortable in asking for [feedback]. . . If you're ever offered a coach, take it. Far too often when African Americans are offered coaches, people get anxious and think that 'They want to push me out.' But that's the best thing they are offering to you, if they are offering it to you out of a desire to help advance your career. White men and white women all the time have coaches. . . Feedback and coaching are really critical, and you should seek it out and you should listen to it."

Paula Sneed
Group Vice President for Kraft Foods

No athlete gets very far in her game of choice without the help of a coach. At some point she needs help mapping out her strategy, or guidance in honing her skills, or simply someone to push her as she practices. Once she reaches her goals, who is the first person she's most likely to thank when she's up on the podium accepting her medal or award?

Her coach.

So what makes you think you can win the career game without the help of a coach? Indeed, at every level of employment, Americans are taking advantage of professional coaching to help them improve job performance and advancement. While it's hard to pin down how many professional coaches there are in the U.S., the International Coach Federation (ICF), a credentialing organization in Washington, D.C., that claims to be the industry's oldest, says it has 7,500 coaches in its membership, up from 1,500 in 1999. A rapidly changing business environment and shortages of talented employees in certain industries are among the reasons credited for this growth.

What A Career Coach Does

A coach is simply someone who helps a client improve performance and reach goals in a desired area. There are many types of coaches used in the workplace, from holistic life coaches to performance-focused executive coaches to team-oriented business coaches. However, if you are looking for help with your climb up the ladder of success (or with deciding which ladder you should be on), then a career coach might be right for you. "It's one of the fastest growing aspects of coaching," says Daniel Martinage, executive director of the ICF.

"A career coach can help you to figure out 'what you want to be when you grow up' or to get off on the right foot in a new job or career," explains Daphne Houston, PhD, career coach and CEO of The WorkDoctor, Inc., in Dallas, Texas. "Career coaches also can help you improve your ability to market yourself inside and outside your company, or to negotiate your salary. If you are between jobs, a career coach can help you search for a job, prepare for interviews, or even decide if you're better off starting a business instead.

"People who seek my career-related services generally want to improve a particular aspect of their career, be it getting a promotion or making a transition to a new field. I help them identify what they are best suited for, what a new career would look like, and how to make a livable, doable plan to achieve their goals," adds Houston.

However, people who seek career advice are often unsure of what they really want to do. "In those cases, a career assessment is often helpful to identify skills, gifts, abilities, and preferences," says Houston. "In other cases," she continues, "people know what they want to do but need coaching to help them form that dream into an actionable plan. They also need someone to support them and hold them accountable for getting it done." The roles for which people rely on their coaches on the most, according to IFC research, are those of "sounding board" and "motivator."

Most personal coaching is performed by telephone, according to the ICF. A typical coaching period is six to eight months. For their services, "experienced coaches and counselors charge $75–$250 an hour for individual sessions. Average charges are in the range of $100–$125, though," says Houston. Some coaches may charge monthly package fees, instead of hourly.

Who Benefits Most From Career Coaching

Despite the cost, career-coaching services are not just for corporate elites. "In fact, those at the mid-level and below are ideal because small changes can make huge differences in their careers. A trend is that companies are increasingly willing to bring in career coaches to work with groups of middle-and-below-level employees—though it's true that at the higher levels employers more often pay for coaching assistance," says Houston.

Minorities are using coaching with increasing frequency, says the ICF's Martinage. The black women who have come to Houston tend to be "proactive" types who are not afraid to seek help in getting ahead, she says. "These are women who seek me out not because they are doing badly, but because they want to do better. The senior executive black women that I've coached need an external ear, and a way to simulate the game with the big boys at the table. They want someone they can relate to, with a global corporate background, so they can plan their next steps carefully with someone they can trust."

Who Your Career Coach Should Be

Finding someone you can trust and with whom you have a good rapport is important, because an effective coaching relationship is truly a partnership. "Make sure you are satisfied with how you relate, that there is a good connection," advises Martinage. "Also you'll want to check their references, find out how long they have been a coach, whether they are credentialed, and what their schooling is in coaching," he adds. Since most coaches will offer a trial session for free (thirty minutes is typical, says Martinage), you'll want to use that time to decide whether that coach is a good match for you.

Also, beware of coaching programs that lock you into a commitment of longer than ninety days unless you know you want to work with that particular coach over the long term, warns Houston. Exceptions can include job search programs and executive-level coaching, she adds.

The truth is, you may need only one session. "I start with single sessions, and aim to clearly identify what we'll work on," she explains. "Then if there is a need for ongoing support we will work together over a 90-day or 180-day period of weekly or biweekly sessions."

To find the right coach for you, check with your human resources department. You can also contact the ICF, visit its website, or consult one of the resources listed below.

Resources

International Coach Federation
1444 "I" St. NW, Suite 700
Washington, DC 20005
Phone Toll Free: (888) 423-3131
Phone: (202) 712-9039
Fax: (888) 329-2423 or (202) 216-9646
Email: icfoffice@coachfederation.org

The Journey Productions
http://www.jenniferlewishall.com
thejourneyproductions@msn.com
Life Coaching and Professional Development

Power Living Enterprises
71 West 128th St.
Third Floor, Suite B
New York, New York 10027-3102
Phone: (212) 289-6363 or (212) 348-1218
Fax: (212) 289-6466 (fax)
http://www.power-living.com

profundities
10 West 15th St., Suite 526
New York, NY 10001
Phone and Fax: (212) 645-3005
http://www.harriettecole.com

**Val Williams Professional Coaching
and Training, Inc.**
118 Coppertree Ct.
Edison, NJ 08820-4054
Phone: (732) 632-9647
Fax: (877) 443-4092
Email: val@valwilliams.com
http://www.valwilliams.com/

The Work Doctor and Associates
15455 N. Dallas Pkwy, 6th Fl.
Addison, TX 7500
Phone: (972) 818-3939
http://www.daphnehouston.com

"Become Your Own Brand"

NIA ENTERPRISES LEADERSHIP SUMMIT,
NEW YORK, APRIL 30, 2004

*"The brand of you is important. It doesn't even have
to be a business. It's just how you navigate your life.
It is important for you to be clear about who you are.
And when you are, the right people come into your
world, the miracles happen, the grace is there, but
it's self-effort and grace."*

Harriette Cole
life coach, author, and syndicated columnist

Heather Davis: If you haven't met me, I am Heather Davis,
vice president of sales and marketing at Nia Enterprises.
I just wanted to do a little testimony.

Perhaps two years ago I was on your side of the table,
and I was in awe of this lady right here. I was so inspired
by her panel in Chicago, and at that time I didn't work
for this company. And so I'm really grateful to be here

and to be able to introduce someone I've admired from a distance, and now she's sitting right next to me.

This panel, of course, is "Become Your Own Brand," and we couldn't have chosen a better person to have that conversation with you. In my line of work, branding is everything. This session will show you why branding should be everything to you, too, no matter what your line of work may be. Conducting it will be life coach, image expert, and writer Harriette Cole.

The evolution of the Harriette Cole brand has led her to become a relationship coach on the ABC Family Network reality TV series, *Perfect Match New York*; a nationally syndicated columnist who advises readers each week about sense and sensitivity; the author of books about African American weddings and personal development, including *Jumping the Broom*, *Vows*, and several others; and the owner of an image business, Profundities, which has counseled celebrities such as Alicia Keyes, Mary J. Blige, and Erykah Badu.

I am so proud, again, to have her on our team as a career issues columnist for NiaOnline. Ladies, I give you Harriette Cole.

Harriette Cole: Thank you and good afternoon. It's so great to see all of you. It's really nice to be invited to talk about being your own brand. I know you're on the other side of this table, but all of you are here for a reason—to learn about personal branding.

I have been working toward creating my own personal brand for a very long time and to be invited to speak as an expert on that subject means that I am achieving some success in that regard. It's important to receive acknowledgment for what you're working toward, because it lets you know you're on the right path.

We can get very disappointed and frustrated and tired when engaged in the work of achieving our goals because our goals are often too diffuse. I recommend to people all the time: dream big and write your dreams down. I'm a firm believer in writing everything down. Imagine what you want to do, and who you can become. What is the greatest you that you can become? Who is she? What does she do? What does she look like? How does she move in the world? What are her values? What does she stand for? That's how you create your own brand. When you answer those questions and then come back and fine tune the answers, they create a whole.

A lot of times we have many dreams and when you try to execute all of those dreams at the same time you dilute your brand. You can do many things at the same time, but it's all in how you do them, and what strategy you use to do them that determines whether or not they will work.

I want to tell you a little bit about my career, to give you a sense of what I have done, and what I am continuing to do, and what has worked for me. But before I do that, I want to tell you about Ralph Lauren, one of the biggest brands in the world.

There's nobody in this room who doesn't know who Ralph Lauren is. Ralph Lauren is a Jewish man who started out as a fashion designer creating American fashion in the sense of what is the most homogenous idea of American fashion. Probably a lot of people don't even know that he's Jewish. He changed his name to a name that sounded all-American and he created a business (using baby steps to make it internationally successful) based on a very clear vision of creating Americana for everyone.

One of the things that is very interesting about Ralph Lauren is that his vision was so clear, and vision is the most important thing. Any Ralph Lauren display in any store must follow the rules of his branding. What do the displays look like? You probably have seen them. If he's doing something for the outdoors, for gardening maybe, even the dirt will be placed in a certain way.

He started out making affordable items, women's couture, and then went on to license everything there is, from sunglasses to paint, from jeans to baby clothes. Some of the first clothes that I got for my baby daughter were Ralph Lauren, and they are some of the finest-quality things. Because everything matches the quality of his vision. That's why it works.

So, I look at people like that. I look at Ralph Lauren. I look at Donna Karan. I look at the people who have won. You could look at Martha Stewart, because she has won, even though she's having some problems right now. She's a winner because her vision is seen through every single thing that is part of her brand.

So how do we do that for ourselves? That's what we all want to know, how can we be Martha Stewart, or someone like that? But that's not really what you want to know, it's really: how can I authentically be me in a commercial society? How can I make money being me, and offering my services to the world?

I was very fortunate. I knew from the time I was twelve years old that I wanted to be a writer. And it's good when you know early what you want to do. I knew I wanted to write books. When I was twelve, I was writing poetry and short stories and hiding them in the closet in my home in Baltimore. I was afraid to show them at the time. I was very shy. I was so shy that I spoke so quietly that people couldn't even hear me. You can hear me now. So any transformation is possible.

I retreated to my words as a way of taking care of myself. And that is why my words have been cultivated to the extent that they provide income for me, for my employees, and for my family. From twelve years old that was my goal.

I was also interested in fashion. So my passions were writing and fashion. I was, when I was young, the tallest, skinniest one. And that wasn't really cool on the playground, but it was very cool in the fashion industry. So I became a model when I was a teenager. I started modeling at thirteen or fourteen. Something about the theater of modeling made it OK for me to be on a stage, even though I was still very shy, so it worked.

Throughout school, I was an English major at Howard University, I was a straight A student. I was very serious about education, I was very much on the social scene, and I was a model, so people knew me. Howard had huge fashion productions.

I went from doing fashion shows at Howard to writing for the *Hilltop*, Howard's newspaper. I wrote a fashion column. The one thing I didn't do was get an internship in college. I'm mentioning this to you because all these things are things you can do now. You can get an internship now in whatever you want to do, so that you can get better.

So I graduated from college, Phi Beta Kappa, summa cum laude, and really couldn't find a job because I'd worked in fashion stores and as a model. I worked for a member of Congress, basically as a secretary, and you can imagine how disappointed I was. I had to wear a blue suit and white shirt and a little tie, and blue pumps, and sheer hose. And I was a fashion girl!

So I created two internships for myself at newspapers in Washington. I convinced the editors to let me write for them for free, so that I could write fashion, so I could get a job in New York. And I called every single person that I met along the way from college, who lived in New York, who worked for a magazine, and said "I want to get a job writing fashion at a magazine, can you help me?"

And that's one of my mother's lessons: treat people well, be kind, no matter what. You don't have to be everybody's friend, but treat people well, because the world is very small, and if you treat people well, that's part of your brand, then they know that you are kind, you are thoughtful, you are respectful. It does come back to help you.

So I called all these people who I knew in New York and said, can you help me get an interview? Not get a job, because nobody can really help you get a job, but I got two interviews, I had my clips, and I was offered two jobs, and the job I took was at *Essence*. Neither job was in fashion, so I was somewhat disappointed because when you're twentysomething years old, you really think you should have everything.

Patience is the most important part of this process, I assure you; patience and focus. Focusing on your vision:

what is my vision? Who am I? Who do I want to be when I move to the next stage of my life and my career? Keep asking yourself those questions and focusing on them, so you have patience and you don't get diverted.

So, I worked at *Essence*. I started in the lifestyle section, and six months after that, I traveled to the Ivory Coast in West Africa. I traveled all over the world while working at *Essence* documenting the cultures of people of African descent.

I quickly moved up the chain. I worked as many hours as there were in a day. I did every extracurricular thing *Essence* asked me to do so that I could learn and grow. I was invited to become the fashion editor, which was my goal, after I'd been at *Essence* for seven years.

I'd kind of given up on that goal, but I knew I'd be working in fashion in one way or another, but it came to me. It came to me at exactly the same time as I published my first book, *Jumping the Broom*, which was published eleven years ago, and has sold over 100,000 copies. I have gotten royalties from that book for eleven years, which is really unusual and significant.

Also, that book became a trailblazer for African American nonfiction books, because it proved to the publishing industry that you can make money on African American authors who write nonfiction.

I got a call from a literary agent asking me to write a book about black weddings. So grace is very important in this process too. And I didn't want to write a book about weddings, by the way, because I was in the middle of a divorce. But I didn't tell them that I didn't want to do it. I knew enough to know that people don't often invite you to write a book.

I had wanted to write a book since I was twelve. At that time I was about thirty-one. *Jumping the Broom* was published when I was thirty-two. It took twenty years for my first book to be published. It wasn't what I thought my first book would be, but it was a book. And it had been published. I had created many wedding stories for *Essence*, which helped me to know what African American women want to know about getting married. And so I knew how to do it, and that's why they asked me to write it.

So, I already had a brand that I didn't know I had, by working for *Essence*, which was the only black women's magazine of any acclaim at the time, and was the only publication doing stories about our way of doing weddings. And I was producing them. I'm telling you this story because this is when the light went on for me.

When my book was published, it was just when I became the fashion editor, and I went all around the country talking about my book. It wasn't *Essence*'s book, it was mine. So my brand then shifted to being me—me identified with *Jumping the Broom*, no more Harriette equals *Essence*, Harriette equaled *Jumping the Broom*.

As I was traveling around with *Jumping the Broom*, people would ask me other questions. Any type of question you can imagine. People believed that I could answer them. Before an audience like this or larger, "Harriette, how do you do X or Y?" And I thanked God for my family. I grew up in a home where we learned every rule of the table. My father was a judge and my mother was a retired kindergarten teacher. Every rule, we knew it. I didn't like knowing it, but now I earn money knowing it. I started answering the questions and I realized that there was a need for a book to help us understand what the rules are and how to follow them.

And that is why I wrote *How to Be*, which is more than an etiquette book. I call it a guide to conscious living for African Americans. Know your history, understand what the rules and morés are, wherever you're going, and make a conscious choice about what you're going to do. When you make a conscious choice, whatever it is, you can stand by it. And so I began to realize that with *How to Be*. I started my business with that book. I left *Essence* after working there eleven years, because we no longer had the same vision.

You might have this experience if you work for somebody else. We started having a lot of friction. I had grown up there. It's a great place, but I didn't equal *Essence* anymore. I was discovering what my brand was. What do I really believe? What specifically do I want to do? And no longer did I specifically want to do that, so I shifted. I started a business that, by the way, came to me in a dream several years before. So dreams, real dreams happen too, write them down. I woke up and wrote it down. Profundities is the name of my business. Why? Because it was in my dream.

And I named my business that, I stood by that name from the first day that I started my business. I met with a businessman who owns a big media company on Madison Avenue, and he said, "Why did you call your business that? Your business should be called Harriette Cole. What does profundities mean? Your brand is your name, your brand is you." But I didn't agree with him. I wanted to hold onto the name of my business, and I did.

However, over the years I have figured out, yeah, you know, my business does exist under that name [profundities], but how people know me is not because of profundities, they know me because of my name. I have a website, and it's called HarrietteCole.com. So, when you get advice, write it down. You may not listen to all of it in that moment, but if you hear it, you will engage it when you're ready. Nothing's going to happen until you're ready. I figured that out.

The people from my office were calling for different things, "Oh, I'm calling from profundities," and nobody really cared. Then, they asked why we didn't use my name. So they started saying, "I'm calling from Harriette Cole's office," and then the doors started opening. And that made me realize, there's value in what I offer, and people are understanding what I do. But it wasn't clear enough. Like friends of mine, people who know me really well, several years ago people would say to me, "I'm not really sure what you do, Harriette." And I was shocked. And the reason is, because I do a hundred things. You heard a few of them.

My column, by the way, came as a result of *How to Be.* When I started my business I made a list of all the things I wanted to do. And I'm doing them one by one, because I've been focused on it. There's focus, and I say grace also. I got an e-mail one day from somebody from a newspaper syndicate saying, "Are you syndicated?" I had been asking the *Daily News* for a year to syndicate my column after they invited me to do it, but the time wasn't right yet. I wrote one day a week. "Well, you should be syndicated," she wrote. I called the woman that day.

Then Ann Landers died, and I became part of a pool of many people trying to get those positions. My column has been syndicated for two years, and now they retired Dear Abby—and my column runs six days a week in the *Daily News*. They retired Dear Abby to put me in there. I think that that's really significant. And the syndicate offers my column all over the country.

Guess where many people are interested? Salt Lake City. Go figure. And I mention that to you to say, I started in black media, most of my books have been written to African American audiences, and a big thing for me was how do I transition to a broader audience? Us and others.

Because I've been fortunate enough to be engaged by the media, I've done a lot of things on television. I did every kind of fashion makeover that you can imagine for years. Gordon Elliot used to have a show on network TV, Leeza, Ricki Lake, I did all of them, fashion makeovers forever, product demonstrations, every possible type of thing. This is why my friends didn't know what I did. Well, you do these things, you do product demonstrations, you write books about weddings, you help to start other magazines. What do you do? What do you *really* do?

And so I had to hone it in. What do I want to do now? And what do I want to tell people that I do? I don't have to say everything that I do. Because if you have your own business, you may do a whole lot of things that other people don't need to know.

I'm speaking the truth. And by the way, I wrote a book called *Choosing Truth*, which is very important. To be authentic, you have to live honestly. It doesn't mean you have to tell everybody your business, but in my book I tell a lot of my business, because I want you to understand how deep you have to go to get to who is authentically you.

Your mother may not like your hairstyle, your mother may not like something about what you choose to do, or your family may not understand. Like when I wanted to leave *Essence* to start my own business I got, "are you crazy?" No. I'm making a choice that is authentically my choice.

Over these years, things have happened to support my vision, from weddings to etiquette, from etiquette to relationships. I hosted a thirteen-episode television series last year, while I was pregnant. I was invited to do that through my column, a British television company contacted me.

I have a child, as you know. You don't stop. If you stop, your priorities change. If anybody has children or you intend to have children, you can have children and make your dreams come true. I didn't know if I believed that, by the way. Because I am not young with a little baby, but I'm glad I have her. I stopped for a minute, sort of.

My column must be written no matter what. A week after she was born I was writing my column. She's in one arm, I'm typing in the other, because it had to be turned in. Two weeks after she was born I was on *The Today Show*. Two weeks after that she was in the green room with my mother and I was on TV. Eight weeks later she was with me in Chicago on *Oprah*, because if *Oprah* calls, you go.

The first time I was on *Oprah* was with *Jumping the Broom*, and people all over the world saw me. And it helped to create my brand. Now my brand has shifted to *Harriette Cole equals helping other people to become the best that they can be.* That is what I do. I do it through magazine publishing, I do it through my column, I do it through books, I do it through television, I do it through speaking engagements. I do one-on-one trainings with people in the entertainment industry, with sports figures, how to be your best, how to communicate who you are effectively and clearly, and how to make money doing it, how to be happy doing it.

That's what I do. And I think a lot of people now understand that that's what I do, because I continue to fine tune it more and more and more. When I was on *Oprah,* people called from all over the country asking me, because Oprah said, if you can solve the situation (it was a really prickly situation) you should have your own TV show. Everybody heard her say that, and television executives called. People flew in from LA to talk to me. They had begun to court me about another show.

I've wanted to have a TV show for ten years. I intend to have one. So along the way, I have my goals, and I write them down. I have my dreams, I write them down. Every single day, I have a list of things, my to-do list, of all the projects that I'm working on, what do I have to do so I can accomplish them. I surround myself with people who are clear thinkers and who are pleasant.

And I tell only what is relevant to whoever it is that I'm talking to. Everybody doesn't need to know my life story. People don't need to know what my dreams are. Because people steal dreams.

When establishing the brand of you, do it, become it, live it, then people will see it. Only talk strategically to the people who can support you. It's really important. Don't pick up the phone and talk to the people who are going to complain and complain and complain. We have all done it. Stop. It's a waste of time.

Know that you can have it all, not just all at the same time. But more important, you can be happy through all of it. It doesn't mean that you always have a lot of money. It doesn't mean that you always have the right staff, or whatever it is that you need. But you can, at the core, be happy if you are pursuing what your heart tells you to pursue.

And in branding yourself, there are a few things, points that I want to make. I have some handouts for you that are all about branding, the definitions of elements of branding. You must be relevant to whatever the market is that you want to be in. If you want to brand yourself with something that nobody cares about, we live in a commercial society, and you want to make money doing it, so you have to figure out, "What are people going to pay you for that you can do?" And it could be anything. People who love being mothers have started daycare agencies and made a lot of money. It could be anything, but you have to figure out how it is relevant to the market.

You have to be consistent in what you put out. If you aren't consistent, then people question your integrity and question your ability to fulfill whatever it is you said you were going to do. You have to build relationships. It's what every mother told us. Be nice to people, talk to people. It's not sucking up to people. It's making relationships, which here today we're all doing.

Form relationships that matter. Everybody whose card you get today may not be somebody who's going to stay in your life. Even if you leave here with one person that you believe you can create a strategic relationship with that's going to matter, not friends, necessarily. We don't need more friends, but relationships.

Another thing that you need is to be mindful of whoever your customer is. Again, it's about practicing kindness and being aware. So if you have a customer base of any kind, and we often start very small, how do you treat people? How do you answer the phone? How do you answer the phone when you don't feel like talking to anybody? It's very important to go out and network and go to events, and it's very good to affirm one thing that you intend to do.

Remember I said don't tell it all—but if you have a lot of dreams in your head and people ask you, "Well what do you do?" you've wasted your energy. You've wasted the moment. Even if you're not doing it yet, you can declare, I am actually working on developing my own television show. I tell that to the people who are the right people to tell. It doesn't exist yet, but it will. And I see that it will. I don't say oh, you know, I think I want to—I talk to teenagers who articulate now, this is what I do, because I'm working towards it now, not what I want to do, what I may do. Be clear.

You can choose one thing, even if you aren't sure if that is going to be the be all and end all. I started out as a fashion model. But now, because I know fashion, my first column on NiaOnline was about fashion. Fashion has sustained me for many years, but there's more than that to what I do. You can grow and expand and become more clear about what it is that your brand means, and articulate that. Every time you have a chance to articulate who is the brand of you, say it. Don't say I'm the brand of me, but say whatever it is.

You keep saying it, you're going to meet somebody who says, oh, I'm interested in that. Let's talk about it. When you talk about it with the right person, you become more clear. The more clear you become, the better able you are to execute your dreams in a commercial society and make money. Does that make sense?

I'm going to have a chance for us to have question and answer, because I'm sure there are specific things that you'd like to talk about, and I'd love to be able to entertain that. So who has questions or comments?

Summit Delegate: I'm so familiar with your work. We're both authors. I love what you do. And your candor today here is so real, I loved it. How did you go about your life coaching? Did you decide to get certification? Do you think it's worth it? What did you do? Where did you go?

Harriette Cole: The question is about life coaching. In my work, how did I go about becoming a life coach? Did I get certification? Is that something that I would recommend? Do I have certification? Nope. And why do I say that I do that now, because that's what people say it's called.

Summit Delegate: And many other people don't, either, by the way.

Harriette Cole: But I think it's important to say to you, sometimes, it's very helpful to have degrees and to have certification in things. I don't have a feeling about it one way or another. For some people it will work. I can tell you one thing, though, whether you have certification or not, if you don't find your audience, it doesn't make any difference.

Where I got it from, people ask me this question—how do you know how to do what you do? Really, it started with my family. I learned how to do just about everything that I do from my parents. I'm really grateful to say that. It really is true.

And then in my travels all over the world, and constantly writing about my experiences, and reading. You can read every book that you could learn in a program, where you get a degree, so you understand how to do it. And I'm not saying don't get a degree or get a certification. It could be helpful.

My first job in the entertainment industry, in coaching a recording artist, came as a result of working on *How to Be*. I was at a cocktail party and Andre Harrell, who was, at the time, president of Uptown Records, which is Mary J. Blige and Jodeci and those, said "What are you doing now?" And I was writing *How to Be*. And *How to Be* is 500 pages, and I was really slowly getting it done. But I articulated, "I'm writing this book." And he said, "Do you think you could do that with my artists?" And I said, "Do what?" He said, "Teach them how to be." I said, "Sure."

I had just started my business, on a dream, with a book contract. I started out doing that, and I have made a lot of money in the entertainment industry, because I've developed my own method that helps people to understand how to clarify the brand of them, and how to articulate it in three minutes, in five minutes. When they're doing a newspaper or magazine interview and people are following them around, that's the harder one.

When you have your down time, what does it mean? When you walk out of your house you are the brand of you. Every day you represent something. What is it?

Another question?

Summit Delegate: I wanted to pose a question from here. Some of us are tracking corporately. And we're not all entrepreneurs. I wondered if you had some advice to share to help us in posturing as a brand, in a career path?

Harriette Cole: I have two sisters who are very high-level corporate executives, and lots of other people in my life that I listen to a lot, to hear how they do it. And very recently I talked to my younger sister, who is an engineering executive. And we were talking about her career path. It's going to the events that matter, putting yourself in the company of the executives you respect, and you'd like to learn from. And when you put yourself in the company of those people, what do you talk about? Know what's happening in the news. Know what's happening with the business. Don't talk about the bad stuff about the business in a public setting.

I mean, people do. If it's in the news, the stock's plummeted, don't talk about that at a cocktail party. But also, don't talk about things that don't matter. Use those moments carefully. Do your research to find out what the jobs are, and what the track can be. Where could you go in your business? Where can you work specifically?

If you make yourself invaluable to your company, you may create your own job. That's one of the things my sister did. She has a title that they never had before, because they value her so much that they said, "We want you to stay, so let's figure out something else." And they also understood, based on what she offers to her business, it was more than what her job was.

Another thing: you have to be willing to work really hard forever if this is what you want to do. Plenty of people just work and do well at their jobs and make money and take care of their families, and there's nothing wrong with that. But if you're creating your brand within your business, you are working every minute. You are focused every minute. You're not talking on the phone to your friends. You're not bemoaning any situation when you're at work. You are on point, strategizing for your next move.

You're not pushing anybody. You're creating relationships that work. If there's a position that you can create because you become invaluable to your business, they will recognize that. But you also have to be careful. In some businesses the boss may not want you as a shining star. You could create the brand of you, and become unemployed. It's happened to a lot of people.

So recognize that there may be another step for you. It may be in another corporation that wants a shining star. It may be you creating a business that does whatever it is you do at your business.

Summit Delegate: How important is copyrighting the name of your company or your website, like buying up other similar domain names and things like that? And I was wondering if you knew the correct process to go about that?

Harriette Cole: You always want to protect your name. And so any way that you can protect your name is important.

It really depends on how much money you have, how much protection you can buy.

A domain name is not expensive. But what's interesting is there are some people who have businesses that are the brand of them, their name, and they can't buy their name because somebody's already bought it. And whoever has already bought it, will negotiate for very high rates in order for you to buy your name back.

My background starts in fashion, there are many fashion designers who don't own their name anymore. For example, Martha Stewart doesn't own her name, her business owns her name, the public owns her name.

I work with an attorney. I have a trademark for Sense and Sensitivity, that's one of the things that I decided from the moment that I had it, when I went national, I went with the trademark. When you get an attorney who understands how to do that, and what happens with trademarks, there's every possible category in the world, and you buy as many as you can.

In order to trademark your name, you wouldn't want to trademark it in every field, but it's about $400 or so for every category, so it's very expensive, but it's worth it.

Summit Delegate: I work at the patent office.

Harriette Cole: Good, so you can explain. Please explain.

Summit Delegate: I work with patents, but I just want to say, there are three ways to legally protect your intellectual property. You can get a patent, which is for like a product; a trademark, which is like for your name, and a logo design; and copyright for whatever you write.

As a patent examiner, I examine applications; I've been working in this field for eight years. I know the importance of securing that protection, because the last thing you want is for somebody to get rich off of your idea. And as Harriette suggested, it is not required to obtain an attorney, but when you don't know what you're doing, we highly recommend that you get an attorney.

Harriette Cole: Even though it's not required, think of it as required. Don't make the mistake of trying to be an expert in areas where you are not. When you don't have much money you try to do everything yourself. Make relationships and barter, create any kind of strategic relationship you can so that it will work.

I'm working on a magazine project right now with another woman, Myiti Sengstacke. We're starting a magazine called *Uptown*. Every single person that's working on this magazine is making pennies. But we believe in it. We trust the people who are doing it. And they couldn't do it if they didn't have me, Myiti, and the other people who are working on it. I don't work on most things for pennies, trust me, I have a family to take care of. But I believe in it and believe that it's going to grow.

You can find people to believe in your vision if it's clear. You can find an attorney to defer payment if you develop that kind of relationship. I work with an attorney now. I've worked with him for twenty years. I met him when he was in law school. When I had no money he did stuff for me for no money, and now I pay him whatever can be paid.

If you want to build your brand, another way of diluting it is thinking you can do everything. Make the relationship so that you are good at what you do, and you have the other people who are on your team who are good at what they do.

Summit Delegate: Say a little bit more about diluting. Was there a moment for you, like a light-bulb moment, where you said this is my brand and I need to let go of doing this and maybe set that aside for some time and I'll come back to it maybe? Talk a little bit about that.

Harriette Cole: It's a continuing process, other people see you and think, oh, she's so successful and everything is perfect. It's not perfect. I'm constantly fine tuning. I've been practicing meditation for thirteen years, and whatever your spiritual practice is, I think it's so important, because you become more clear about who you are, and then you can do anything in your life better.

So through that process, I began to see more clearly what matters to me. What do I really care about? And somewhere along the way, probably about five or six years ago, it became very clear to me that I believe my purpose on this planet is to help myself and others to discover how to be their best. I really do. I think that's why I'm here. And I'm very good at that.

And we all have gifts. And if you pay close enough attention to how people respond to you, when the magic happens, then you can figure out what your gifts are. I feel really blessed to know that, and how do I package that? How do I turn that into something commercially viable? That happens in different ways.

It was a tricky thing to move from fashion to that, because that's bigger. It's been a very tricky thing to move from an African American understanding of that, to broader. And I'm still in that process. The question still comes up, "Well, but you only talk to black people." But I'm talking to you, so what do you mean?

I also regularly consult with people who know more than I do on different topics. So as I now am working to create this television project, I've talked to people who really know. I now have an agent through William Morris, which is one of the biggest talent agencies in the country, they came to me. So grace is a big part of this, you do a lot of work and then the grace comes, and you recognize it. You have to recognize when it's a great thing that's there.

So, I talked to them because they know, and I teach them who I am. I tell them names, like a big title now is life coach. And the point that you said about degrees, there was a project that I was recently considered for, a very big television project, and I didn't get it. They loved me. They wanted me. They said we want you to be there. And the reason I didn't get it is because I don't have a therapy degree.

So that's the only reason. I don't claim to be a therapist. I'm not, but I help a lot of people. And they wanted me but they were afraid, because I didn't have the credentials.

So, times come when you don't have something that you need. I recently met with a woman who said to me, "Don't say all the things you do." She reminded me, "You don't have to say all that. If your biggest goal is this, that's what you talk about." And you need to have as much presence in mainstream media as possible, so that's what I'm doing, creating those relationships.

Summit Delegate: It almost sounds as though you have this statement that is you, this is what I'm about, and then these other things that come to you, like is that in line with that vision?

Heather Davis: I wanted to just comment. I have this burning need to say something that I learned that changed my whole perception, and it's in support of everything that Harriette has just imparted.

I had somebody tell me to write a mission statement for myself. And I kept—I could not figure out how to write a mission statement for myself. This is just a sound bite, but I decided when I was challenged like that, to decide on one thing, so as not to dilute and to focus, and then go after that and then if I see any deviations along the way, to pay attention, have peripheral vision about it too.

And my mission statement was really simple and stupid, but it worked for me. It still does, by the way. I want to be the consummate sales and marketing professional. That's my career mission statement, and it works. So I just wanted to give a little testimony to that. And it is working, by the way.

Harriette Cole: And there's something else that I didn't mention that is very important. And I told you my background is fashion so how you look is very important. People look at you from head to toe, front to back. I can't tell you how many people have on the flyest outfit, and their heels are all eaten up on their shoes. I'm not going to look at your shoes, but if you are one of those people, get them fixed. Seriously.

Since Katie Couric got on *The Today Show* wearing fly shoes every day, people pay attention to shoes more than ever before. How you look makes a huge difference.

As you get older, you have to stay young, because we live in a youth-driven culture. So as you get to your forties, it means something else. You get to your fifties, and most people are dead meat by the time they get to be fifty. It's a horrible fact. The way to stay real and current and make an impact and make money, is to stay fresh. So figure out what your style is, and every time you leave your house look like what you say you do.

Summit Delegate: Depending on the field . . .

Harriette Cole: You determine whatever it is. If you work in corporate America, don't go to work looking like you work in SoHo and wonder why you got fired, or why you didn't get promoted. The whole thing about dressing down, if nobody else wears jeans to your job, why do you? If you're trying to be the high-level executive, what does that look like?

Remember that you look like the brand of you. People that know me know that I've always had different hair. My hair has always been a signature, and my glasses. The fact that I change my hair and have a funky hairstyle, and I just had a baby, it works for me. People say, "You just had a baby? What? But you still look cool." You know.

I can tell you, just as many people would say "What did you do to your hair?" I don't care, I decided that I want to look the way I look and stay fresh, and I've made a choice, and I'm very strategic. No matter what happens in your life, that's what you need to do for the brand of you. It's paying attention to every detail, because when I look at you, when you look at each other, you're sizing each other up whether you mean to or not.

Heather Davis: Would you say there's—I don't know if I'm asking or answering the question right now—but I think there is also some merit to having a role model in all of this.

Harriette Cole: A role model or mentor would be great. If you recognize somebody who does what you want to do, and you can create a relationship with that person, great. It doesn't often happen though, because they can get jealous. "You want to do what I do? Uh uh." Or, if they're really working very hard at it, they may not have time.

So that's why internships are very important. Volunteer for somebody who does what you want to do, and really offer your service and do your very best, even if you don't end up working for that company, you learn. Create relationships with people who know more than you. And it may be three or four relationships, because you want to know about different things. And when you create those relationships, don't squander time. Most people you want to talk to are busy.

So, when you communicate with them, do it in a time-sensitive way, and figure out how you can both benefit from the relationship. Every communication that you write, make sure it is grammatically correct. I'm serious. Make sure that you spell people's names right. So many people spell my name wrong. If you don't care enough about me to know how to spell my name, why should I care about you?

All of those details are really important. They make the difference. When you take the time to pay attention, and when you're upset, that person, that role model, is somebody who will keep your confidence. You do need a sounding board that's not somebody at your job, that's not somebody who has a big mouth, that's not a negative person. It's somebody that's going to say, "OK, I'll listen to you now, and let me inspire you to be positive again."

Heather Davis: Would you say that in your journey you saw the need to purge people?

Harriette Cole: Absolutely.

Heather Davis: Change neighborhoods?

Harriette Cole: My book *Choosing Truth*, which I recommend to you because it will help you to get to the core of you. In that book, there's a chapter called "Keep Good Company," all the things that your mama told you.

I've made choices to let people go. I don't always tell them, but I stop calling them, writing to them, communicating with them. Anybody who you keep trying to be friends with doesn't need to be your friend. Anybody who, every time you talk to them they're negative, you don't need to talk to them anymore. People who don't treat you the way that you want to be treated, this is the golden rule, it's all core stuff. I'm not creating anything new, I'm just reminding us.

Yes, I've let people go. And I'm much better at it now than I used to be. I used to hold onto people for a long time, "Please like me. Come on, please. Let me give you one more reason so that you can understand why you should like me, why you should value me." I did it when I was a little girl and it hurt my feelings, I did it as an adult and it hurt my feelings. I don't do it anymore.

When I feel it, I say OK, I don't have enough time for that, goodbye.

I had dinner the other evening with a well-known journalist and his wife. He said that at a certain point, he realized he did not have to keep people in his life. So he has told people, "I don't want to ever talk to you again."

He said he was just frank. He wasn't mean. He was clear. He told me two specific people with whom he had this conversation or this statement. And it made you laugh and think. Some of you may think, "How horrible." But it's much worse to pretend to be somebody's friend and talk about them behind their back. And many of us have done that. It's much better to just say, "You know what, let's not talk to each other anymore." I wouldn't say it the same way he did, but direct is better.

Summit Delegate: Several times you referenced strategic relationships when you talk about mentoring and how you use that to promote the brand of you, because yes, you can do it, but doesn't it help more when you have other folks also promoting your brand? And how do you go about getting them to promote it the right way, as opposed to dilution?

Harriette Cole: That is the reason why I say whenever you have an opportunity to talk about what you do, be clear about what you say. You know advertising works because they say the same thing over and over again. Everybody knows who said "Just Do It." Why do you know that? Because it's said over and over. *Mine is helping you to be the best you can be.* You all will leave here probably remembering that, because I'm telling you, *what I do is to help people be the best they can be.*

I bet some of you will tell somebody else that, even if we didn't have this conversation. So you keep saying what it is that you do. Someone said to me once, "Figure out how to describe what you do in the time that it takes to ride on an elevator." So, use the principles of advertising, read about advertising and marketing and branding. There's tons to read about it.

And what I have for you is definitions of branding that you can read. It's more concrete. And you talk to people in your church, and wherever you are in your community. If you work in corporate America, talk to human resources, talk to your boss. This is what I intend to do. This is what I'm good at. Remind your boss of what you're good at. Because we're constantly putting out there who you are, what your brand is, you keep stating it. That is what every advertiser does. Why? So that you will recognize their brand.

Also, you can advertise in books or events, the sororities' conventions, dinners, all kinds of things where you can put an ad in. They're often very affordable, and put an ad in saying what you do. In black newspapers, if you're trying to reach an African American audience, just put an ad in the newspaper.

As you grow, depending upon what it is you do, find a way that you can advertise what you do. Keep putting it out there, so people will understand what you do.

Heather Davis: We have time for one more question.

Summit Delegate: I have Harriette's books, they're wonderful. They make wonderful gifts. Because developing our brand, thinking about our brand, reinforcing our brand, is so time consuming, it's important work and it's good work, but how do you find time, unplugged, to keep finding that center of yourself?

Harriette Cole: I meditate. That is what I do. I have a very active spiritual life. I told you about my list that I make every day. On my list I also put drink water, eat, meditate. Because I used to not remember to eat. And that's not good. Many of us who are working very hard don't take care of our bodies.

For years I would get a massage every Friday. I didn't necessarily always have the money, but I made sure that I could do it. Now I have a trainer. I just had a baby. I've got to get fit again. So I do that. I don't want to wake up in the morning extra early to do anything, but I do it because I have my vision, I have my goals for what I'm going to do.

So make a list. I highly recommend it. Write down on your list what you're going to do. That way you can keep track. You don't have to hold it all in your brain, and include taking care of yourself in it.

If you have a partner, make sure you pay attention to your partner, because you won't have one otherwise. It's very important to pay attention to your whole life. Branding is hard. Everything's hard. What's not hard? Branding ultimately makes it easier because you become clearer about what you want to do, and therefore, other people do too, and so your world becomes more concise.

I do encourage all of you to take it seriously, no matter what you do, the brand of you is important. It doesn't even have to be a business. It's just how you navigate your life. It is important for you to be clear about who you are. And when you are, the right people come into your world, the miracles happen, the grace is there, but it's self-effort and grace. Everything is hard.

But it can be hard and fun. It can be hard and fabulous. It's your choice. My life is fun. I work with people who are kind and friendly and I choose to spend my time in the company of people who are supportive of me and others. You can make that choice too. Sometimes you work with people in which that's not so, but friction is important for change. You can thank the people who really make you mad. If you ever get fired from a job, you can thank them because you got pushed out to do what you're really supposed to do.

Everything negative can become a positive if you think about it long enough to figure out what the good is, what's the lesson? I don't have to do this again. You get the lessons until you learn them. You know how you got remedial school if you failed something; you had to keep taking the class until you got it right. Life is the same way, you just don't always think about it like that.

I don't want to have to get lessons over and over. I want to learn it and move on and get a new one. Thank you.

PART 4

CREATE YOUR OWN
OLD GIRL'S NETWORK

11

NETWORK
Your Way To Success

"I love to participate in any type of session where you are working and networking with women. I always tell people that it is always very comforting. We know it. We know each other, or we have a natural affinity."

Reta Lewis
Vice President and Counsel to the
President of the U.S. Chamber of Commerce

It's easy to mingle if you're a social butterfly. You can strike up a conversation with strangers and keep track of old colleagues without breaking a sweat. But what if you're the shy type? With the right amount of know-how, you can still learn how to network and step out of your comfort zone, according to Frederica J. Balzano, PhD, and Marsha

Boone Kelly, coauthors of *Why Should Extroverts Make All the Money? Networking Made Easy for the Introvert* (Contemporary Books, 1999).

Whether you're the belle of the ball or usually hanging with the wallflowers, the important thing is knowing the right way to schmooze and establish a network. "Networking is not only about putting on the power suit for a business lunch, shaking hands, and giving people business cards," says Peter Vogt, president of Career Planning Resources, a career-counseling firm in Eden Prairie, Minnesota. "It can simply involve talking to someone about your interests and asking questions—whether the guy up the street, the person who cuts your hair, friends, or family members."

So what is networking? For one, it's the process of strategically cultivating relationships around common interests. Making the right connections can help you identify customers for your business, secure money for graduate school, or land a new job or promotion. In fact, according to career statistics, more than 60 percent of jobs are found through networking, and up to 90 percent of openings are filled by word of mouth.

Networking is also a skill, points out Patreece M. Thompson, a consultant with Career Concepts in Birmingham, Alabama. "You have to be able to strike a balance between gathering information from people, interviewing, attending meetings, and having quiet time to sort out the data and decide what you want to do and how you'll achieve the goal."

If you have recently found yourself without a job, now is a great time to make use of this tool by asking members of your network to let you know when they hear of any opportunities that might suit you. And be sure to check out these expert tips on effective networking.

Here are some simple networking dos and don'ts:

Establish informal and formal networks. Each week, make an effort to talk to two people in your company you don't usually talk to; each month, try to talk to two outside of the company. Widen your circle of contacts by meeting others in your profession and community. Attend a business social or association meeting. Consider volunteering to work the registration table at a conference or event.

Keep track of people. Maintain regular contact with friends, family, acquaintances, and all those people you promised to keep in touch with. Foster connections to your alma mater and alumni groups. Keep a record of each person you phone, email, or write, and when you contacted him or her. This way you'll know when you should follow up.

Don't be embarrassed to ask for help. Can you recall the number of people you've assisted without expecting any compensation? Probably not. It's OK to ask for others' assistance. If you recently lost your job, don't be afraid to ask for recommendations or references from mentors and colleagues with whom you have built a rapport. Most people understand the corporate-downsizing cycle. If, for some reason, you have never been particularly altruistic, now may be a good time to start. Consider volunteering your time and talents to a cause that you find interesting, or one that will help you enhance your skills. Getting involved in newfound community or professional activities could turn you on to job leads.

Stay focused on your goals. The next time you take someone's business card, think about your motivation. Is this someone you find interesting and just want to get to know better, or can this person provide important business leads? Jot down on the back of the business card why you want to contact this person again and how you can follow up with him or her. Consider others' needs. Be on the lookout for information that can help your personal and professional contacts. Say, for instance, a contact mentioned that she was interested in buying an electronic organizer. Send her a copy of the article you recently read about the latest Palm handheld computer, along with a follow-up note.

Find ways to connect. Try to meet with people in their offices. Because people are busy, look for ways other than lunch to stay in touch. If you do decide to meet someone over a meal, try breakfast or dinner so that person's workday isn't interrupted.

Show your appreciation. Get in the habit of sending a quick email, postcard, or brief letter to let people know you are thinking about them. One good idea: birthday and anniversary cards. Also, it doesn't hurt to send a small token of your appreciation, such as a bouquet of flowers or a plant. Show others that you are genuinely interested in them.

As you develop your own network, remember that professional relationship building is a lot like dating—it takes time.

Networking *Smarts* Quiz

Are you a savvy networker? Take the Networking Smarts Quiz to find out if you're more likely to be well connected or misdirected. Answer questions one to six without peeking ahead to the answer key on the following page. Then use the key to determine your score, and read the profile that corresponds to your score.

1. **The point of networking is:**
    a. Finding out what others can do for you.
    b. Finding out what you can do for others.
    c. Building mutually beneficial relationships.
    d. Keeping a high profile.

    Score _____

2. **A networker's most useful tool is:**
    a. Her business card.
    b. Her smile.
    c. Her eyes and ears.
    d. Her gift of gab.

    Score _____

3. **The most effective networks are:**
    a. Full of movers and shakers.
    b. Full of up-and-comers.
    c. Focused on the gatekeepers.
    d. Mixes of achievers, aspirers, and gatekeepers.

    Score _____

4. Your networking efforts are most productive:
   a. When you have a goal in mind.
   b. When you have something big to offer.
   c. When you're among the right people.
   d. All of the time.

   Score _____

5. The best networking opportunities are:
   a. In business card exchanges with people from various fields.
   b. At professional networking events within specific fields
   c. At private clubs and exclusive parties
   d. Everywhere you go

   Score _____

6. The most appropriate time to follow up with a new contact is:
   a. As soon as you have something that may be of interest to that person.
   b. As soon as you need something from that person.
   c. Immediately after your initial meeting, with a card, email, or telephone call.
   d. After a week or two, so that you don't seem too eager.

   Score _____

   Total of all six scores _____

SCORING KEY AND PROFILE

Question 1: a = 2 points; b = 3 points; c = 4 points; d = 1 point

Question 2: a = 1 point; b = 2 points; c = 4 points; d = 3 points

Question 3: a = 2 points; b = 2 points; c = 2 points; d = 4 points

Question 4: a = 2 points; b = 2 points; c = 1 point; d = 4 points

Question 5: a = 2 points; b = 3 points; c = 3 points; d = 4 points

Question 6: a = 3 points; b = 1 point; c = 4 points; d = 1 point

If you scored 1–9 points: Bet you've got a sharp-looking business card—but perhaps you're too focused on form over substance when it comes to making connections. There's more to effective networking than exchanging business cards or being seen in all the right places. Focus more on building lasting relationships based on common business interests and mutual benefits.

If you scored 10–14 points: You are probably very goal-oriented in your networking activities, perhaps to a fault. Do you notice that when you call up your contacts you're frequently getting voicemail? Be careful: in the long run, people tend to avoid those who only approach them when they want something. Maintain your contacts even when there's no short-term benefit (remembering birthdays or sending holiday greeting cards is a good, neutral way to stay in contact) and remain aware of how you can benefit those within your circle.

If you scored 15–19 points: You've got the basics of effective networking down, and probably have a solid network of contacts. If you want to take it to the next level, though, try to look for networking opportunities in not-so-obvious places. For instance, twenty floors down from the CEO's corner office suite, the security guard watches everyone come and go. Do you know his name?

If you scored 20–24 points: Congratulations! You are a savvy and effective networker. You rarely miss a moment to make a new contact or strengthen an existing one. You understand that business relationships should be mutually beneficial over the long term, though in the short run they don't have to be a quid pro quo. Can we have your card?

Resources

**National Directory of
African American Organizations**
Altria Group, Inc.
www.altria.com/naad

Career Concepts Inc.
140 West Germantown Pike
Plymouth Meeting, PA 19462
Phone: 610-941-4455
Fax: 610-941-0267
http://www.cciconsulting.com/

"Enjoy *the* Climb"

NIA ENTERPRISES LEADERSHIP SUMMIT,
NEW YORK, APRIL 30, 2004

"Joy is a higher level of knowing that there is nothing that I could be paid to have this moment taken away. Joy is knowing that I finally have peace doing what I'm doing and it feels good....You have to find those moments. But you will know them when they come. And I think you'll say it goes beyond just the job that's going to put me there or a commute that's going to be shorter. It is really an intense feeling that says, 'Even if my commute is going to be hell tomorrow, I have joy and peace today.' So that allows me to deal with all the crap."

Jennifer Lewis-Hall
Emmy-nominated Journalist and Life Coach

Many of us believe that in order to get ahead we have to endure a little bit of suffering, pay our dues so to speak. But at the end of the day, is it possible to overpay your dues?

During the Nia Enterprises Leadership Summit in New York, we explored that question in a panel discussion. Among the experts to address it were Emmy-nominated journalist and life coach Jennifer Lewis-Hall. To follow are portions of that discussion.

Sheryl Huggins: We've got personal development experts who are here to tell you that enjoying your climb up the ladder is as important as getting to the top. They're going to share their secrets for finding happiness along the way as you climb. And they're going to address how you can find a satisfying balance between your work life and your personal life, make an effective career plan that you'll enjoy implementing, and get greater satisfaction from your current work situation.

Jennifer is president and CEO of The Journey Productions LLC. And you may recognize her because she's also an Emmy-nominated journalist, motivational speaker and author of the book, *Life's a Journey, Not a Sprint*. Currently Jennifer is seen on many television network programs and also heard frequently on national radio broadcasts. As a correspondent at CNBC business news for four years, she provided in-depth market coverage throughout the business day and filled in on the anchor desk for NBC syndicated shows, including *Early Today* and *The Wall Street Journal Report*.

She holds a master's degree in journalism from Northwestern University's Medill School of Journalism and a bachelor of economics and finance from Douglass College at Rutgers. She's also one of the youngest women ever to be inducted into the Douglass Society at Douglass College for outstanding achievement. She's currently working on her second book.

Sheryl Huggins: Jennifer, you wrote a book, *Life's A Journey, Not A Sprint,* which I think is a very interesting phrase, about how to achieve success even when you're stressed and overwhelmed. Please touch on what inspired the book.

Jennifer Lewis-Hall: I really think that it's been a collection of my entire life experiences. Let me tell you a little bit about my real life and then about my professional life. Did you ever feel like you're just a title that you have, or that's how people perceive you? Then at other times you also say, "OK, then I go into a quadrant where I'm just the wife, or I'm just the mother."

I started to look at my life in these years as a collection of all those pieces, and how powerful it is to have all these different components in my life and how to use them effectively and interchangeably, professionally as well as personally.

Too many times I think that we compartmentalize who we are and what we do. So when we go to work we become solely the accountant, the business executive, the teacher, or the nurse. We do not draw upon the collection of experiences.

I've spent twenty years in the journalism business. I've worked for publications from *The Wall Street Journal,* to, of course, the NBC network and now WCBS as their work and lifestyle expert—many years in this business in different capacities. And I'm a mother of two sons, ages six and thirteen, and I'm a wife of one husband. I have had a lot going on in a short amount of time. And it occurred to me that you really need to draw upon all of that, not only for strength and prosperity but also because you are so well-versed in so many things. We women don't realize how skilled we really are and how exceptional we are at what we do because we created multitasking. We are the ultimate multitaskers. Yet we compartmentalize who we are. When you have drawn upon your ability to be able to handle five things in one morning—many times our male counterparts are not trained to do that, or do not do that, or do not choose to do that—then you realize really how successful you can be.

I often times tell people that your home is almost like a business that you run, whether you have other people in it or not. Imagine the things that really encompass your life and how effectively we tend to handle them 365 days a year. To manage this "first corporation," you're managing inflow, outflow, business, money, funds, and schedules. You're making it efficient and you're making it happen.

Think about using the tools that you have, just like those on your job. And when you think about how effectively you care for others, and how you get to work, come home and do all these things, and you're part of organizations, and you come to enrich yourself like this at conferences, really, the success that you can have is limitless.

Life's a Journey Not A Sprint was a collection of my life experiences: why it's important to constantly feed your soul, nourish your body and your mind, and have smart tools for success. And what I did was I interviewed and queried women across the country, all ages, all backgrounds, many of them African American women, to talk about what their life experience was and what their keys to success were despite hurdles and adversity. And the commentary really just drew me to tears so many times because people were so honest and poignant. You found that so many of our young women not only had had so much pain early on, but also were so strong.

So I looked at this as a collection of experiences about how we can use our resources and thoughts to get ahead. And, of course, I interviewed some of the top women in business about career success and tools: How do you accomplish these things? Are you having water cooler conversations? That's what I call it in this book: are you going to the water cooler to find out what's up? Too many times we're expecting somebody to come to our desk to talk to us, to tell us that our whole department's about to be let go. Are you having the conversations that are going to get you ahead? Those are not going to require you to be seated in your cubicle, but to navigate a system that's like an office party, which requires you to have a different type of face altogether. It's not being a phony—it's being effective. So what are some of the tools to really get you ahead? Based upon my own experience, every time that I have risen through the ranks in my career I have found that it has had less and less to do with what I know than with

How does your work make you feel on an average day?

Fulfilled   57 (19%)

Stressed out   78 (26%)

Eager to get ahead   61 (18%)

Depressed or angry   18 (6%)

Excited   13 (4%)

No way in particular   73 (24%)

Results of a July 2004 online poll of 300 members of NiaOnline's Consumer Advisory Panel. All respondents were black women eighteen and over.

who I know, and the timing and where I am and how effectively I use those moments.

Having the solid foundation, the education, is a blessing and a gift. But I also know that as you fluidly move through your individual settings, clearly it's going to be important to develop the skill that you use in all of these personal relationships. Being effective at that is going to be key to getting to the next level.

Sheryl Huggins: Let's talk about sacrificing. The truth is some sacrifices are important, you know, as we climb the ladder or do whatever it is as we go down our path to our goals. So what I'd like you to do, Jennifer, is talk a bit about how we choose the sacrifices that we're going to make without sacrificing our total enjoyment of life. How do we choose the sacrifices that are necessary to get us ahead?

Jennifer Lewis-Hall: I think it has a lot to do with how you look at the things that matter. I talk a lot about prosperity but not without priority. And that's because we have seen what has happened all around us. I mean, pick a subject, pick a headline. It has a common theme so often about being prosperous but not prioritizing. And when that happens it all falls like a house of cards.

I mean just recently with, with our athletes and with so many people who we aspire to be like or who we recognize as having greatness, if the priorities aren't there a lot of times the prosperity means absolutely nothing. And when you look at Wall Street—Wall Street is built, really, just on trades. Trades are based simply on the give-and-take of saying, "I agree to pay you this based upon this." But if you don't have the trust and you don't have faith in that institution or that company, it crumbles like a house of cards. And that's exactly what has happened to Wall Street over the past several years because of what? Integrity. It all fell apart.

So a lot of times I think that when we look at the sacrifices that we're making and we think about the priorities in our own lives and how prosperous we want to be, it ebbs and flows. I see now my life transitioning into something different again as my children grow and get a little bit older and their needs change. I all of a sudden say to myself, I have this newfound freedom a little bit, but a huge amount of responsibility a lot. Because now they're going in to become young men, and the commitment needed is going to be even more fierce on some fronts. So what does it require of me? What does my commitment need to be now? I think reshaping your commitment will help you to determine what the sacrifices are that you need to make at the time. A lot of times people will say, well, how do you get into this business? How do you get into television and production? And, you know, it's such a multidimensional platform now. Publishing, advertising—they're linked but they all fall under one broad umbrella. It is competitive and it is hard to do, but what sacrifice at that time are you willing to make? And in the beginning stages, the sacrifice is going to be great. The sacrifice is going to be a lot of what another speaker was talking about, about having butterflies in your stomach, hopefully before you find your health failing. But clearly people will sacrifice just about anything in the beginning stages of that career.

But can you afford to do that? What other responsibilities do you have? That's why prosperity and priorities always need to come into play. You might set yourself up to say, "You know what, I'm going to give this new-found career track eighteen to twenty-four months. I'm going to set myself on a track and see if I can prosper doing this for these two years, but I'm going to sacrifice some of the luxuries that I would normally have because I'm going to move into New York City and cut down on my commute. That means I'm going to have to sacrifice having a car, having disposable income."

But suppose all of a sudden you decide, "I want to add a mate to this equation. I also want to have a healthy relationship. I'm now onto phase two. How do I want to sculpt this so that I have—it's not even the best of both worlds—so that I have a thriving relationship and so that I have time to spend with this person? So now, how am I going to advance that?" And it goes on and on and on as you grow and your life expands.

So you have to determine, I think, in making those sacrifices, how much does something mean to me at this time in my life. Because, interestingly enough, I think we both must feel that at this point there's some things we don't want to sacrifice—

Sheryl Huggins: Absolutely.

Jennifer Lewis-Hall: —right now. You know, I don't want to sacrifice not eating for three days, traveling for two of those, having live shots in front of the White House, and not getting to my son's play, because my first priority in these years is to make sure that I'm there to hear him hit all the worst notes, the best notes, be off-key, be on-key, or whatever it is. Because I have said this is a priority and I'm willing to sacrifice my entire career! [Laughter]

But at the same time, how do you set up other things in your life to balance that? It's interesting, you will see in forums like this that so many people have started their own enterprise because the balance is there, the contacts are there, the knowledge, you know, is intact. So now how can I put that balance into play? I want to have my professional life. I'm not willing to sacrifice my personal relationships or myself. And so, it's a constant pendulum swing. It's constantly saying, "Where am I now? Am I willing to sacrifice these things? And what is the priority to me?" And you'll never go wrong.

Sheryl Huggins: How do you get over guilt, though? When I say this I know especially in this city, there's almost a feeling that you know, "I didn't work ten hours [Laughter] and, you know, boy, if I did, then I'm a good person. In fact, I'm better if I'm working twelve." It's almost a machismo where people almost compete—"Oh, I only got one hour of sleep last night," "Oh, I got half an hour." How do you get out of that guilt of that you've been slacking off?

Jennifer Lewis-Hall: I think you think about your male counterpart. You think about maybe men in your life. I can talk to my thirteen-year-old son and there are just certain things that he does not feel guilty about yet, over which I could be consumed with guilt [Laughter]—the fact that these pants are lying on the floor and the room is going to be a disaster and isn't the world coming to an end? And he's kind of like, "You know, Mom, no, not really." [Laughter] Right?

Sheryl Huggins: Right, right.

Jennifer Lewis-Hall: He's already caught on to the fact—as early as four, five, six, somehow the male genome very quickly catches on to that fact, that, "What's the problem? I'm still going to get up in the morning. I may wear those pants and I'm going to feel pretty good." I used to drop them off at kindergarten and the little girls would run over to me and say, "Mrs. Hall, Joey doesn't eat his lunch and he doesn't wear his coat." And I thought to myself, "My, at four years old you've got an idea of responsibility." He's skipping along throwing rocks and having a ball, and you're consumed your whole recess period about whether he's got a coat on.

Now fast-forward that tape twenty years. We're still worried about many of the things that are not going to get us ahead, that don't really matter in the scope of real life. We all will develop good home training, we're all good home teachers, so in the end we'll all get the rules. But it's funny about how you go about them. And that is a key lesson, because that little girl from four to twenty-four will have been worried about many things that don't matter, that will cause her stress, and that boy will feel great and confident and will be getting a lot of help along the way. That someone may, in fact, be putting his coat on for him. I mean I don't know how far this thing went. [Laughter] But now my youngest son tells me that girls are cleaning out his desk—and he's five years old! It's like, "Well, so and so will help me."

Because the idea is that if you believe this whole guilt thing and you foster it, it's a killer, it's stressful. We as women are consumed with guilt and it robs you of your passion and your dreams. Because you will always feel like, if I'm not giving two thousand percent in this job, in this cubicle, then I'm not going a good job. But guess what? The person sitting next to you is already focusing that energy into getting ahead.

So, a lot of time while you're working on this wheel for twenty hours, you should be working smarter, not working harder, and saying, "You know what, I don't want to use my energy that way." You really have to whip yourself into saying, "I will not allow guilt to consume my life." Because it is a terrible thing and I think that many of us suffer from that as a condition. It stops you from wanting to travel, it stops you from wanting to go back to school. I'll feel guilty if I'm not there at 3:00 p.m. at the bus stop. If I missed the bus this morning I felt guilty. Why? It doesn't make a bit of difference.

So think about how you can work smarter, not necessarily always harder, because that's not necessarily going to get you ahead. And think about how guilt will really rob you of that which you want to aspire to be and to do. Because part of that success quotient is going to be rejection. It is going to be fear, and it is going to be people saying no. But it only requires one yes. So many times people say, "Well, I'm afraid and I'm guilty to try something new and I don't want to go back because I don't deserve it," or, "I don't deserve this time to myself." What is it, fifteen or twenty minutes to take a break at work and have a cup of coffee or a cup of tea?

Tell people, "I need this time and I need this time to myself and I'm not going to feel guilty about it." Because you can be a better person, a better parent, a better friend, a better lover, a better whatever by having it. Otherwise that guilt can be focused and channeled into anger and then that goes into being bitter, and then that goes to resentment. Right? Because we're angry that we didn't get what we really wanted. How many times do people say, "I could have done, I could have been," because they really felt guilty about pursuing something that they really wanted to do?

Summit Delegate: I look at my mother and her peers who are kind of the "first women," you know, the first post-civil rights generation, and they're such amazing women and have overcome so many things. I have this conversation all the time with friends: our moms dealt with the really bad stuff, so you kind of minimize or play down the things that you're dealing with. And so when I joke with my friends, I'm like, "I'm running from one nervous breakdown to another." [Laughter]. How do you get off this stress treadmill? I mean, I'm working full-time, going to school full-time, and having a relationship and all that stuff. Is there a break?

Jennifer Lewis-Hall: What do you like to do? What are some of the things that bring you joy?

Summit Delegate: Reading. I made a very conscious career switch from working in something that I hated—investment management—because I was like, "Why make a lot of money for people who already have a lot of money?"—to publishing, because I love to read.

Jennifer Lewis-Hall: Is that working? Is that helping to reduce the stress in your life?

Summit Delegate: No, it's actually creating a lot more. It's not as difficult to get up every morning but it's just, there's this dichotomy, I'm feeling very pulled in different ways.

Jennifer Lewis-Hall: For us women, even through a twenty-
or thirty-year span, a lot has happened. You talked about
the struggles of your mom's peers and our struggles. If
you're in a room with daughters and the mothers, there
is this feeling, that, "Well, we did this and, girl, we tell
you." And my mother's here in the audience, so I'm not
telling stories. They had this get-up-and-stand-strong
mentality. Because that is exactly what that generation
had to do.

But I think now that when we recognize some of our
contemporary struggles, there is something that's different. We are now dealing with a higher expectation-
level in the corporate world. That is something that our
mothers aspired to do but never quite got there in mass
numbers. We're still not there in mass numbers, but
clearly we're all in this room here today and we've seen
the fabulous accomplishments and glass ceilings broken
by African American women. So we know we can do it,
we are there, and we are now working toward the next
young ladies who are going.

But you can't generationally say, "They struggled,
therefore I can't feel bad." You, in the end, are not your
mother. This is a different time and you and your peers
all chose different avenues. You have clearly determined
what makes you happy and what completes your life. And
people don't really know what brings them joy. They're
quick to say something, but they really haven't thought
carefully about what really brings them joy.

Joy is a totally different place than saying, "I'm happy
right now at this moment." That's what I have found. Joy
is a higher level of knowing that I finally have peace
doing what I'm doing and it feels good. It could be sitting

in your apartment and saying, "You know what, this is the kind of morning sunrise I wanted to see for ten years and never saw." You have to find those moments. But you will know them when they come.

And I think you'll say, you know, it goes beyond just the job that's going to put me there, or a commute that's going to be shorter. It is really an intense feeling that says, "Even if my commute is going to be hell tomorrow, I have joy and peace today. So that allows me to deal with all the crap." Because that's how it is. When you live here, that's what it's going to be like. We're in traffic, we're doing this, we're looking for the next job, our companies are shutting down. But when you have the dichotomy of joy and peace in your life, you say, "You know what, that is what I do, that's not what defines me. This is my life."

Summit Delegate: I want to thank you for your openness in being here with us. I teach physical education. I went into it after being a nurse because I wanted my weekends off. My mother suggested it as the only profession that gives you the weekends off. But I've come to love the profession of teaching. It was just what I should have done [Laughter], but I don't know how I would have gotten into it if not for the issue of weekends, of thinking about myself.

As I see the youngsters today in my charge, both boys and girls, they seem to be playing by certain rules of the game. And I try to tell them life is not a game. You have to take time for yourself, you have to sit back and plan.

Jennifer Lewis-Hall: It's a huge undertaking. It's every moment of the day. I commend you because our teachers in our schools, no matter where they are and how educationally sound they may or may not be, teachers are having to take on the roles of parenting at every pass. So I commend you because you're concerned about their well being, not just their educational experience. But at the same time, these kids are pretty sharp, you know. I hate to underestimate them because they really do get a lot of things. There's one common theme that I try to share with teenagers, particularly those from the younger end of the spectrum—even eleven, twelve, thirteen, as well as nineteen—that "I have an expectation of greatness for you." And that expectation can mean so many different things, but so many of us forget to have an expectation.

We never talk about why I expect something of you. It's not to be heavy—it's to say that you're here for a purpose and also you've got a contribution to make, and I expect you to find it and make it. And there's no other way around that, and that contribution may be so profound and so simple that you never know what it's going to be. And each one of us has that responsibility and will have the greatness in us to do that.

And it's kind of amazing when all of a sudden you turn the tables on them. You know, most people think, well, kids are kids. They're all bad, they're listening to this bad music, everything in the world's going to hell. First of all, these are going to be the people that are going to be taking care of you, managing your money, and running the world in a mere twenty years. So all the bad kids that are always bad end up being either Bill Gates or Bob Johnson from BET or something. And sometimes they just end up being the solid rock of our community, or great parents, because they're going to be something.

But the thing that you have to instill is that "I expect you to be great. I know you can be great and I'm not going to take less than that. That greatness transcends into different things. But whether you want to be an artist or whether you want to work in your community or whether you want to be a decent citizen and role model, that's great. And so find that greatness. But I will not believe that it's not possible." And I think that that's just the common theme. It's simple, they can wrap their arms around that, and they can say, "Well you know what, somebody expects something of me." And even in terms of offices, at Goldman Sachs, on Wall Street—they expect you to perform. So if you start performing early, you will perform later in life. Because that's what every company expects you to do, that's what the Leave No Child Behind Act expects you to do. And don't ever forget it.

Sheryl Huggins: A question?

Summit Delegate: I just lost my job of twenty years. But it just dawned on me the other day, I don't have a job. I have to look for another job. But in the meantime, when I walked out of the office, I said, "Don't look back." And this is the first time really in my life that I can rediscover who I am, what I want to do. I've been a caretaker, a mother, a wife, you know, I've worked in my businesses and worked my job to a point where my health—I was sick all the time, my skin was breaking out, I barely had enough time to sleep. The phone was always ringing, "I need you to do this, I need you to do that. Can you, will you?" and I did.

And it's like, "Now what am I going to do?" You've got to think fast, you know, you have to be on task. Especially being older now. You feel like you're competing with this generation, my daughter's generation, for things. So I've really got to narrow down the niche that I want to fit into and that's what I was going to ask you. How do you do that without so much fear? I think that you just said it all, you know, a lot of prayer, a lot of meditation, being dedicated to what you want to do. And so that right there was like a source of comfort, so I thank you for giving me that.

Jennifer Lewis-Hall: Remember, faith and fear cannot coexist. And that has been such a powerful message for me lately. Because fear will overcome you and it will sap your progress. I'm living this right now. You are right on point when you talk about the age differential and the competition in the work place. You're speaking about real factors. This really exists today. So you have concerns that are justifiable.

You need to be smart in terms of how you want to make the next move. And you have to just take pause to say, "You know what, I have twenty years of solid experience behind me. And no matter what, that is still extremely marketable." But focus that and channel it with the next step. Think about how you can live a lifestyle that will allow you to incorporate your years of work experience, but also have an income.

Money is an important tool. Money is still a tool that we need. So, we need to be smart about how we make decisions, we need to be prudent when we're not working so that we can figure out how to make sure that we have the lifestyle that we want to live. And you do feel stressed out when you know that you've got to make some of these big decisions. But by working your way through them, a piece at a time, it will help alleviate the stress. And you also need to say, you know what, I have an opportunity here.

Summit Delegate: Right.

Jennifer Lewis-Hall: How am I going to use it?

Summit Delegate: Thank you.

Sheryl Huggins: We have time for one more question.

Summit Delegate: I wanted you to talk a little bit more about transitions. I feel like I'm in a bit of an identity crisis right now. Just had a baby eight months ago, got married a year and a half ago, just bought a house in the suburbs. And like, who the heck am I? [Laughter] I was this person who did a lot of great things in media. But now I'm at home mostly and working as a freelance writer and trying to figure out, well, where do I want to go? I don't necessarily want to go back—that was so much for who I was. I'm not quite sure who I am now. So, I guess I'd love to hear you talk a little bit more about letting things bubble up and allowing things to happen and being in a transitional phase to get to the next place.

Jennifer Lewis-Hall: As you have just become a parent, I think that there's two things that I recognize in you. And that's that you're smiling, there's an amazing smile on your face. But then your eyes were saying, "Whoa, this is like really different." And then the smile on your face is telling me that there's a lot of really good and new things that are going on. People think that when you stand at an altar and you say these words, that they mean so much. But acquiring that role is very different. And then all of a sudden, you know, you're also identified also as your child's mom. Many people will never know your name again. [Laughter] Right? "Hi, mom." That's what the kids say.

Summit Delegate: Or as your husband's wife.

Jennifer Lewis-Hall: Right, exactly. And people don't realize that sometimes, you know, you're so happy to have your family, but there's also a feeling of, well, you know, I was me, and I was important, and people did respect my opinions, and they didn't just drop stuff on the floor or whatever. That means that there's some different roles going on. And those roles are going to be going on for a long time.

So to hold on to yourself is something that I think is profoundly important for women in changing roles. And by that I mean hold on to the things that also make you, you. Because if you don't, a lot of times nobody else will. And you'll be recognized and loved and, you know, Mothers Day will come, all these things. But I oftentimes tell people, if you want to wear your hair the way you want to wear it, wear it. If you want to, say, "You know what? I love writing and I want to hold onto part of that because it's what makes me, me."

Because I found that everyone has said, "Mommy, I don't like what you're wearing." "Mommy, do this." "Well, why did you buy this?" It's like, hold it. I bought this 'cause I like it. And it may look crazy, but I like it. Right? And it doesn't mean that I'm not a good person or parent or whatever. Or if my spouse, you know, has a hard time accepting that I went through these crazy hairstyle phases. I know he can't stand it. But it's me. So, in the scope of things, you know, a lot of people will change everything. Then they'll get on the phone with their girlfriends: "Girl, if I could just go to that concert." Go to the concert! And take him if he wants to go.

Hold onto you. Because part of the transition, you're thinking, is, "Hold it, put the brakes on. All of a sudden everything that I know has changed." But when you take those pieces that are you—that funky dress that you love, or that music you like to play when you get in the car—it's you. Embrace you.

Make it a point, I think, to get out and foster yourself in your business when you can, whatever it is you're doing, because I've found that when you keep that toe in the water, it keeps you fresh and you can move fluidly when you decide. We forget that all of a sudden they're going to go to first grade and have a full day. Many women have said, "Well now, everybody's gone, what do I do?" Or, "I feel like I am so steeped in their lives I do not have one of my own." That is not a good thing. You are here as an individual being. You deserve it, you owe it to yourself; people love you because you're you.

12

HOW TO TAKE ADVANTAGE
of **Mentor Relationships**

"I cannot stress enough the importance of mentors and the need to take to heart the advice and guidance they provide. My mentor, the phenomenal Ann Fudge [Chairman and CEO, Young & Rubicam]... taught me the importance of integrity and balance as the keys to well-being and success. . . To this day we still keep in touch; in fact, at my wedding she cried more than my mother."

Candace Matthews
President of SoftSheen-Carson

There's a great quote: "Learn from the mistakes from others, because you won't live long enough to make them all yourself." Mentors who have "been there and done that" are wonderful resources; they have a great wealth of knowledge and experience in their professions. Better yet, they impart—for free—their wisdom to help you with day-to-day career decisions.

Many of the sisters involved with Nia Enterprises seminars and summits describe advancing through their careers thanks to the counsel of trustworthy mentors—both male and female, African American and other. Some have been ongoing, while others have been momentary. No two relationships have been the same, but all have been enriching.

It doesn't matter what you do for a living—everyone needs a mentor now and then in order to get ahead at work, pursue higher education, or start a business. A mentor can be a friend or a colleague who can serve as a support system. Good mentors take a personal interest in helping others succeed. They also know that mentoring is about developing people, not fixing them.

Mentoring has evolved over the years: it used to consist of an old boys' network in which a senior male executive would anoint a younger version of himself as his protégé. The relationship was built on chemistry, commonality, and connections—the mentor who was several rungs higher up on the ladder would steer the lower man toward career-enhancing projects and plum assignments.

Women, however, weren't able to form personal bonds the old-fashioned way, on golf courses or in cigar bars; nor

> **Have other black women helped or hindered you in the workplace?**
>
> **Mostly helped me** 85 (28%)
> **Mostly hindered me** 44 (16%)
> **Helped and hindered me equally** 85 (28%)
> **Neither helped nor hindered me** 85 (28%)

Results of a July 2004 online poll of 300 members of NiaOnline's Consumer Advisory Panel. All respondents were black women eighteen and over.

could they expect men to pick them as protégés. But now there are "girls' clubs" at work that are helping women learn the skills they need to be successful. Women Unlimited is a New York-based professional-development company devoted to mentoring, education, and networking. Dispelling some common myths, Women Unlimited has come up with its "new rules" for mentoring:

Old rule: Mentors and protégés should have a lot in common.
New rule: The best matches are mismatches.

Old rule: You should look for your mentor higher up on the food chain.
New rule: A good mentor is anyone you can learn from.

Old rule: Mentoring is one-on-one.
New rule: Mentoring works best when you mix and match.

Old rule: Mentors pick their protégés.
New rule: Protégés pick their mentors.

Old rule: You are either a mentor or a mentee.
New rule: Everyone needs mentors.

Women Unlimited matches a group of mentors and protégés who are selected by their respective companies to participate in the program. Similarly, The Ladies Club 2000 offers an online mentor-network program.

Take advantage of grassroots mentoring programs. Contact women's organizations, professional associations, or trade groups to find out if they offer mentoring as part of their professional-development programs.

Of course, you don't need to belong to a formal group to find a mentor. You can seek out on your own anyone from anywhere inside or outside of the workplace. Some friendly advice: pair up with someone who is different from you—meaning of another sex or race—so that person can challenge you. Moreover, seek out more than one person. Bottom line: you need to develop a way to learn from the people around you.

Sometimes it is better to give than receive, so be sure to think of what you can offer your mentor. A sister just starting out her career can offer grunt work. *New York Times* reporter Lena Williams has recalled how she offered baby-sitting services to her mentor, CNN South Africa bureau chief Charlayne Hunter Gault. People are more likely to help folks who don't appear needy and who aren't just trying to get without giving in return.

Resources

The Ladies Club 2000.com
Cynthia Jones
P.O. Box 60333
Las Vegas, NV. 89160
http://www.theladiesclub2000.com/

13

MENTORING GIRLS—
Creating
the Next **Great Success**
Story

"My really, really big thing is the importance of just taking a young person under your wing. For me, it's like breathing. But it's also a way to ensure your legacy."

Terrie Williams
Publicist and Founder of The Stay Strong Foundation

Finding a mentor is really only half of the game of creating your own "old girl's network." The other half lies in being a mentor yourself and helping to guide a new generation of black women down the path of career success. Without sisters who are willing to provide that guidance, each successive generation of young black women will be forced to learn the same lessons over and over again. As was stated in the introduction to this guide, nearly half of the minority women corporate managers who participated in a 1999 Catalyst study cited the lack of an influential mentor or sponsor as an impediment to their success.

On an individual level, a protégé can provide a base of support for her mentor early on. Additionally, her success could someday put her in the position to be of professional assistance to her mentor.

Mentoring doesn't need to begin in the workplace, however, or even with adults. From a very early age, "girls need role models and exposure to people and professions with whom they may never come in contact in their daily lives," says Diane Tukman, who is director of collaborations and adult support for the Girl Scouts of the USA. "How else will they learn and grow?"

A common excuse that adults use for not mentoring young people is that they don't have the time. "Mentoring can take as little or as much time as you have to offer,". insists Tukman. "It's important to be realistic about the time you have to give. Mentoring might be conducted in person or online, on a regular basis or a few times a year."

Making sure that you match your interests to the right opportunity, organization, and mentees are crucial to your success in mentoring. "There are some national mentoring organizations that through the internet will help you make the connection that matches your interests with those of a girl," advises Tukman.

Below is a list of organizations through which you can mentor girls or connect with the right mentoring organization:

Girl Scouts of the USA helps girls build character and gain skills for success in the real world. Nearly 1 million adult

Are you a mentor to someone?

Yes I am currently
86 (28%)

No but I have
been in the past
107 (36%)

No I've never been
a mentor
107 (36%)

Results of a July 2004 online poll of 300 members of NiaOnline's Consumer Advisory Panel. All respondents were black women eighteen and over.

volunteers—from troop leaders and trip chaperones, to guest speakers at troop meetings—are helping nearly 3 million Girl Scouts to develop strong values, leadership skills, social conscience, and conviction about their own potential. Activities include community service projects, cultural exchanges, clinics for building athletic skills, environmental stewardships, and other such learning opportunities. Web: www.girlscouts.org. Telephone: (800) 478-7248.

Big Brothers Big Sisters of America, founded in 1904, is the oldest youth mentoring group in the country. Its programs bring together adult volunteers and children, most of whom come from single-parent families. Activities with your "Little Sister" might range from going to movies or museums, to helping with homework, to just taking walks together. To find out about volunteer opportunities, go to the website and search for a local affiliate. In this case, the ability to give a steady amount of your time is essential. Web: www.bbbsa.org. Telephone: (215) 567-7000.

Boys & Girls Clubs of America, which has been around since 1906 (although girls were not recognized in the organization's name until 1990), is one of the country's largest mentoring organizations. With celebrity alumni ranging from Jackie Joyner-Kersee to Queen Latifah, Boys & Girls Clubs have given millions of American children a safe and fun place to learn and grow. More than twenty-five national programs are available in the areas of education, the environment, health, the arts, careers, alcohol/drug and pregnancy prevention, gang prevention, leadership development, and athletics.

Sixty-five percent of members are from minority families, and 44 percent are female. Visit the website to find a local club where you can volunteer. Web: www.bgca.org.

Girls Incorporated is a network of 1,000 affiliated organizations through which girls ages six to eighteen participate in programs that deal with violence prevention, teen pregnancy, sexuality, media images, community service, leadership, and career development. Programs such as Discovery Leadership inspire girls to lead by pairing them with women leaders. Web: www.girlsinc.org. Telephone: (800) 374-4475.

iMentor matches young people from underserved communities in New York City with adult volunteers via schools, after-school programs, and other community organizations. The nonprofit matches youths with adults who have similar career interests. Mentors and mentees email each other regularly, meet in person a few times each semester at iMentor-sponsored events, and collaborate online on projects designed to improve students' reading, writing, research, and technology skills. Web: www.imentor.org. Telephone: (718) 923-2852.

MENTOR/The National Mentoring Partnership works with schools, businesses, churches, and youth organizations to support the expansion of mentoring opportunities. It also links mentoring agencies, and interested adults to mentoring organizations. Its website includes a locator that searches by ZIP code for mentoring organizations in your area. Web: www.mentoring.org. Telephone: (703) 224-2200.

Ask Yourself:
What Kind Of Mentor Should I Be?

Your success as a mentor will depend upon the finding the right opportunity to fit your interests, schedule, lifestyle, and skill set. Before you volunteer, take a few moments to answer the following questions. Use your answers as a guide when you assess a mentoring opportunity.

1. Do I prefer dealing with young people in groups or one-on-one?
2. Do I have a schedule that permits an ongoing, regularly scheduled commitment, or are one-shot activities more realistic?
3. In which manner would I prefer to keep contact with a mentee: in person, by telephone, by email, or by written correspondence?
4. What am I interested in teaching or sharing with a young person?

Recognizing The Brown Angels In Our Lives

Every year, Nia Enterprises gives awards to people and organizations that have supported the growth of black women and girls in business and civic life. Furthermore, NiaOnline regularly profiles individuals who are making a difference in our community.

Below is a list of individuals who have been recognized as Brown Angels since our founding:

BROWN ANGEL INDIVIDUAL PROFILES (2000-2004)

Hattie Anderson: breast cancer survivor

Dayton Brown: Interstate Realty Management

Della Clark: Enterprise Center

Emma Creamer: Pastor of Cathedral of Fresh Fire

Arlene Fletcher: food bank volunteer

Kevin Gillespie: U.S. Army sergeant

Suzette Harper: Children's Hospital of Philadelphia's TLC Program

Monique Hunter: Food From the Hood

Leonard Johnson, D.O.: Spruce Adolescent Counseling and Education Center

Joyce Keener: Human Potential Consultants

Gladys Knight: singer and founder of Elizabeth Knight Fund

Angela Maxfield: Conway Regional Health System

Julia McGinnis: HIV/AIDS peer counselor

Bonita Parker: Salem Baptist Church's
Financial Ministries

Evelyn Parker: food bank volunteer

Eva Paterson: Equal Justice Society

Julieanna Richardson: HistoryMakers

Joyce Roché: Girls Inc.

Victoria Rowell: actress and founder of
Rowell Foster Children's Positive Plan

Pernessa Seele: Balm in Gilead

Mychal Sledge: Sledge Group Consultants

Maggie Smith: Pastor of Walking in the Word Church

Claudia Stevens: Black Women in Fire Service

Ann Stringfellow: family caretaker

Launa Thompson: Clear Channel Communications

Terrie Williams: Stay Strong Foundation

BROWN ANGEL ORGANIZATIONAL PROFILES (2000-2004)

Athletes Against Drugs

Community/Ecumenically Concerned Helping Others

Dress for Success

Ecofaith.com

Mocha Moms

Reach to Recovery

ShiNE

Sisters Network

The Tavis Smiley Foundation

Women's Self-Employment Project

BROWN ANGEL AWARD RECIPIENTS

Link Unlimited: 2002 Award for Outstanding Leadership in Community Diversity

DaimlerChrysler: 2002 Award For Outstanding Leadership in Business Diversity

Steven Rogers: 2002 Leadership Award

City Year Chicago: 2003 Award for Outstanding Leadership in Community Diversity

Carol Moseley Braun: 2003 Award For Outstanding Commitment to Promoting Leadership Among African American Women

Northern Trust : 2003 Award For Outstanding Leadership in Business Diversity

Kraft: 2004 Award For Outstanding Leadership in Business Diversity

Melody Spann-Cooper: 2004 Award For Outstanding Commitment to Promoting Leadership Among African American Women

Merri Dee: 2004 Award For Outstanding Leadership in Community Diversity

Barack Obama: 2004 Award For Outstanding Commitment to Promoting Leadership Among African American Women

LEADING LADIES ON
Success *and*
Significance

"And when you think about how effectively you all care for others and what you do and how you get to work and how you come home and you do all these things and . . . you're part of organizations and you come and enrich yourself like this—really the success that you have is limitless."

Jennifer Lewis-Hall
President and CEO of The Journey Productions LLC

If you've come this far along in your reading of this book, you're certainly committed to doing what it takes to achieve career success on your own terms. But do you have what it takes to go to the next step? Do you have what it takes to lead?

Historically speaking, it's not a question that has been posed to African American women very often. Despite a legacy of behind-the-scenes leadership within the church, as well as during the abolition, anti-lynching, and civil rights movements, black women have rarely been perceived—or perceived themselves—as people with the qualities and mandate to lead.

But all you have to do is observe the greater frequency with which black women leaders are grabbing headlines in the national media—U.S. National Security Advisor Condoleezza Rice and media mogul Oprah Winfrey are a couple of high-profile examples—to see that sisters are slowly moving to the forefront of corporate and civic leadership ranks. Trendwise, it's still a trickle at this point, but it's a significant crack in the dam that has held back our leadership potential for generations.

The unique challenges and triumphs experienced by leading sisters were explored during the May 2002 Nia Enterprises Leadership Summit held at the Kellogg School of Management, Northwestern University in Evanston, Illinois. The theme of the summit was "From Success to Significance," and over the three-day period hundreds of African American women who are successful by whichever yardstick you choose gathered to explore how they can derive more meaning and satisfaction from their accomplished lives.

In preparation for the conference, we at Nia Enterprises asked a couple of prominent sisters questions about the nature and responsibilities of leadership. The women we spoke with included:

* **Dr. Barbara Ross-Lee,** who was the first African American woman to head a medical school (Ohio University College of Osteopathic Medicine) and who is now dean of the New York Institute of Technology's New York College of Osteopathic Medicine.

* **B. Smith,** syndicated TV host, style expert, and entrepreneur.

* **Bonita Parker,** personal investment expert and national director of the 1,000 Churches Connected initiative launched by Rainbow PUSH.

Here is what they had to say:

NiaOnline: Which qualities separate a leader from someone who is merely successful?

Smith: True leaders always think before they feel. They analyze a given situation, see the benefits and risks associated with it, then act. Furthermore, they move forward, bringing with them all the resolve necessary to accomplish the task at hand. They never act selfishly and always take the high road. True leaders refuse to project the negative and always promote and strive for the very best.

Parker: The primary difference between a leader and someone who is successful is that leaders are visionaries, not by conforming to consensus, but rather by molding and empowering others to participate in a common goal for the greater good of an institution or community. Successful people tend to excel in the execution of goals; however, they are more driven by individual accomplishment and conformity rather than by empowerment and broad based achievements.

NiaOnline: What is the number-one responsibility of leadership and how have you applied it to your own life?

Ross-Lee: You must establish a vision and facilitate the achievement of that vision through effective communication, continuous quality improvement, innovation, and the use of excellence as the basic standard for all activities. Personally and professionally, I have established a vision for myself to make a positive difference in everything that I do by being the best that I can be and doing the best that I can do.

NiaOnline: As a leading black woman, do you feel an extra responsibility to be a role model?

Smith: I believe all human beings are intrinsically role models, for good or bad, affecting and influencing future generations.

Ross-Lee: Absolutely! My gender and race, in a very real way, contribute to and detract from all of my efforts to accomplish specific goals. Therefore, my achievements communicate to the community at large not just success, but the fact that success can be achieved by a black woman in a traditionally white-male-dominated professional arena.

It is important that women and minorities are aware of the possibilities. Every successful example demonstrates that the glass or concrete ceilings have been and can be breached. I feel a personal responsibility to maintain and widen that breach so that our daughters and sons can get through. Being a role model means reaching out, including, promoting, supporting, and engaging the next generation above and beyond my personal job description.

Resource Bank

Nia Enterprises/NiaOnline

23 West Hubbard St., Suite 200

Chicago, Illinois 60610

312.222.0943

Fax: 312.222.0944

Email: info@niaonline.com

http://www.niaonline.com/

CAREER RESOURCES

Alert Staffing

Corporate Office

300 Corporate Pointe, Suite 300

Culver City, CA 90230

Phone: (310) 665-9380

Fax: (310) 665-9390

http://www.alertstaffing.com

Catalyst

120 Wall St., 5th Floor

New York, NY 10005

Phone: (212) 514-7600

Fax: (212) 514-8470

Email: info@catalystwomen.org

http://www.catalystwomen.org/

JobStar

http://jobstar.org/

The Ladies Club 2000.com

Cynthia Jones

P.O. Box 60333

Las Vegas, NV 89160

http://www.theladiesclub2000.com/

NAACP
4805 Mt. Hope Dr.
Baltimore, MD 21215
Phone: (877) NAACP-98
24-Hour Hotline: (410) 521-4939
http://www.naacp.org/

WetFeet, Inc.
609 Mission St., Suite 400
San Francisco, CA 94105
Phone: (415) 284-7900
Fax: (415) 284-7910
http://wetfeet.com/

Workforce America
Candidate Resources, Inc.
2100 Hwy 360, Suite 400-B
Grand Prairie, TX 75050
Phone: (972) 641-5494 x199
Fax: (972) 641-5647
Email: mcotter@criw.com
http://www.workforceamerica.org/

PROFESSIONAL TRAINING & COACHING

Career Concepts Inc.
140 West Germantown Pike
Plymouth Meeting, PA 19462
Phone: 610-941-4455
Fax: 610-941-0267
http://www.cciconsulting.com/

Novations/J. Howard & Associates
Brighton Landing West
10 Guest St., Suite 300
Brighton, MA 02135
Phone: (617) 254-7600
Fax: (617) 254-7117
Email: info@jhoward.com
http://www.novations.com/

Tulin DiversiTeam Associates
5 Curtis Park Dr.
Wyncote, PA 19095-2211
Phone: (215) 884-7325
Fax: (215) 886-5515
Email: info@diversiteam.com
http://www.diversiteam.com/

**Val Williams Professional
Coaching and Training, Inc.**
118 Coppertree Ct.
Edison, NJ 08820-4054
Phone: (732) 632-9647
Fax: (877) 443-4092
Email: val@valwilliams.com
http://www.valwilliams.com/

NETWORKING

The Five O'Clock Club
300 East 40th St., Suite 6L
New York, NY 10016
Phone: (800) 538-6645 x600
http://www.fiveoclockclub.com/

International Coach Federation
1444 "I" St. NW, Suite 700
Washington, DC 20005
Phone Toll Free: (888) 423-3131
Phone: (202) 712-9039
Fax: (888) 329-2423, (202) 216-9646
Email: icfoffice@coachfederation.org

LIFE COACHES / LIFESTYLE EXPERTS

Power Living Enterprises, Inc.
71 West 128th St.
Third Floor, Suite B
New York, NY 10027-3102
Phone: (212) 289-6363 or (212) 348-1218
Fax: (212) 289-6466
info@power-living.com

PUBLIC SPEAKING AND PRESENTING

Toastmasters International
P.O. Box 9052
Mission Viejo, CA 92690
Phone: (949) 858-8255
http://www.toastmasters.org/

MENTORSHIP

Girls Inc.
120 Wall St.
New York, NY 10005-3902
Phone Toll Free: (800) 374-4475
http://www.girlsinc.org/

DIRECTORIES OF BLACK-OWNED BUSINESSES

**National Directory of African
American Organizations**
Altria Group, Inc.
120 Park Avenue
New York, NY 10017
Phone: (917) 663-4000
http://www.altria.com/responsibility/04_04_04_01_africamerdir.asp

**National Association of Colored
Women's Clubs and Youth Affiliates, Inc.**
1601 R St. NW
Washington, DC 20009
Phone: (202) 667-4080
Fax: (202) 667-4113

ECONOMIC EMPOWERMENT

**1000 Churches Connected
(Initiative of the Rainbow/PUSH Coalition)**
Rainbow/Push Coalition - 1000 Churches Connected
930 East 50th St.
Chicago, Il 60615
Phone: (773) 373-3366
Fax: (773) 373-3028
http://www.1000churchesconnected.org/home.htm

U.S. Equal Employment Opportunity Commission
1801 L St. NW
Washington, D.C. 20507
Phone: (800) 669-4000
Phone: (202) 663-4900
http://www.eeoc.gov/

CREDIT RESOURCES

Equifax Credit Information Services, Inc

P.O. Box 740241
Atlanta, GA 30374
Phone: (800) 685-1111
http://www.equifax.com/

Experian

Phone: (888) 397-3742
http://www.experian.com/

TransUnion

P.O. Box 2000
Chester, PA 19022
Phone: (800) 888-4213
http://www.transunion.com/

Consumer Information Center

Consumer Information Catalog
Pueblo, CO 81009
Phone: (888) 878-3256
http://www.pueblo.gsa.gov

Federal Reserve Board

Division of Consumer and Community Affairs
20th and C Sts. NW, Mail Stop 800
Washington, DC 20551
Phone: (202) 452-3693

Federal Trade Commission

Credit Practices Division
600 Pennsylvania Ave., NW
Washington, DC 20580
Phone: (202) 326-3650

National Foundation for Consumer Credit

801 Roeder Rd., Suite 900
Silver Spring, MD 20910
Phone: (800) 388-2227

READING LIST

The Millionaires' Club: How To Start And Run Your Own Investment Club—And Make Your Money Grow
by Carolyn Brown (John Wiley, 2000)

Having It All? Black Women and Success
by Veronica Chambers (Doubleday, 2003)

Choosing Truth: Living an Authentic Life
by Harriette Cole (Simon & Schuster, 2003)

How to Be: A Guide to Contemporary Living for African Americans
by Harriette Cole (Simon & Schuster, 2000)

Having What Matters: The Black Woman's Guide to Creating the Life You Really Want
by Monique Greenwood (Amistad Press, 2002)

Your Gift Will Make Room for You
by Daphne Houston, PhD (Houghton-Miller, 2003)

Shifting: The Double Lives of Black Women in America
by Charisse Jones and Kumea Shorter-Gooden, PhD (HarperCollins, 2003)

Life's A Journey—Not A Sprint: Navigating Life's Challenges and Finding Your Pathway to Success
by Jennifer Lewis-Hall (Hay House, Inc, 2004)

Volunteer Slavery: My Authentic Negro Experience
by Jill Nelson (Penguin, 1994)

Success Never Smelled So Sweet: How I Followed My Nose and Found My Passion
by Lisa Price and Hilary Beard (Random House, 2004)

Thrive! 7 Strategies for Extraordinary Living
by Felicia Scott (Butterfly Works, 2003)

**Seven Soulful Secrets for Finding Your Purpose
and Minding Your Mission**
by Stephanie Stokes Oliver (Broadway Books, 2001)

**Success Gems: Your Personal
Motivational Success Guide**
by Jewel Diamond Taylor (Quiet Time Publishing, 1999)

Stay Strong: Simple Life Lessons for Teens
by Terrie Williams (Scholastic, 2001)

**The Personal Touch: What You Really Need
to Succeed in Today's Fast-Paced Business World**
by Terrie Williams with Joe Cooney (Warner Books, 1996)